Parasha Meditations
For Spiritual Renewal and Strengthening
Communication with the Creator

Book Three: Vayikra
Online with Hashem

Rebbetzin Chana Bracha Siegelbaum

Midreshet B'erot Bat Ayin

ויקרא

Vayikra

Parasha Meditations
For Spiritual Renewal and Strengthening Communication with the Creator
BOOK THREE: *Vayikra* Online with Hashem

פניני מדיטציות בפרשה :
מדיטציות מקוריות להתעוררות רוחנית וחיזוק הקשר עם בורא עולם

Published by Midreshet B'erot Bat Ayin:
Holistic Torah for Women on the Land
Text Copyright © 2017 Midreshet B'erot Bat Ayin

COVER DESIGN: Chana Bracha Siegelbaum and Meital Helfon
ART WORK: Yenta Leah Guzzi
GRAPHIC DESIGN: Meital Helfon and Chana Bracha Siegelbaum
TYPESETTING & GRAPHIC ADJUSTMENTS: Ruth Simchi
EDITING: Devora Gila Berkowitz

Midreshet B'erot Bat Ayin
The Village of Bat Ayin, Gush Etzion 90913, Israel
Tel: 972.2.993.2642 | Fax: 972.2.993.1215
Email: info@berotbatayin.org | www.berotbatayin.org

ISBN-13: 978-1544857442
ISBN-10: 1544857446

Printed by CreateSpace, an Amazon.com Company
To order additional books, please email info@berotbatayin.org

Other Books by Chana Bracha Siegelbaum:
Parasha Meditations: For Spiritual Renewal and Strengthening Communication with the Creator: Bereishit & Shemot
The Seven Fruits of the Land of Israel
with their Mystical & Medicinal Properties
Ruth: Gleaning the Fallen Sparks
Women at the Crossroads:
A Woman's Perspective on the Weekly Torah Portion
The Nameless Chicken from Judea   (A colorful children's book)

Dedications

I dedicate this book to the *aliyat neshamah* (soul elevation) of my *Zeideh*, my father's father, Israel Leib Vainer, born February 10, 1890 near Dvinsk in southeastern Latvia. I regret that I never got to know my Zeideh very well. I remember him only as a silent patriarch with a mild nature, sitting modestly in an armchair at the corner of the room, in his own world. Although he was fluent in Russian and Yiddish, his Danish was quite broken, limiting communication with this quiet man even more. Thanks to my father's detailed memoirs, I have learned more about my Zeideh and his background. He immigrated to Denmark in 1908 and met my *Bubby* there five years later, when she was only 17. They married the following year. My grandfather worked diligently as a shoemaker at a shoe factory and later opened his own shoe store in the center of Copenhagen. It was important for Zeideh to be well-clad and work himself up in society. He earned a gold medal at the Scandinavian Trimming School, for fine trimming and fit. Zeideh had plans to immigrate to America, and had saved up for a whole year to pay for the fare.

In 1917, he departed for the trip with his brother Meier. Yet, it was not meant to be. While his brother set foot in the United States, Zeideh was detained at Ellis Island and returned to Denmark due to his impaired eyesight. Thus, it came to pass that my father was born in Denmark, while many of his cousins are American.

*M*ay Hashem bless Rebbetzin Chana Bracha with much success to spread Torah with health and happiness always!
- Nili Segal, N. Miami Beach, FL, USA

*I*n the *zechut* of the *ilui neshamot* of my dear parents, Yitzchak ben Elazar Dov and Chaya Bryna bas Mordechai Dovid, a"h. May they be *zoche* to *techiyat hameitim*!
- Shalomis Koffler Weinreb, Baltimore, MA, USA

*I*n loving memory of our Dottie with love always
- Sarah Elisheva and Rachel Hadassah, Dallas, TX, USA

L'ilui nishmas Avram Shneur Zalman & Rivka Gilman, Eliezer Peretz ben Avram Shneur Zalman & Slava Gilman, Dovid and Basya Smith, Reuven ben Dovid, Lenore Smith & Elaine Smith.
– Basya Ruth Gilman, N. Miami Beach, FL, USA

*I*n loving memory of Gital Chaya Chana Rachel bat Bracha Yetta. May her *neshama* have an *aliya*!
 - *Laynie Stern, N. Miami Beach, FL, USA*

*I*n loving memory of our father, Laibel ben Hershel and our mother Chana bat Eliezer OBM, who both passed away this past year. With love from their daughter and son in law Chaim and Leah Batya Lizer.
– *Henry and Laurie Lizer, LA, CA, FL, USA*

*I*n honor of my husband, Calev Zachariah for being unconditionally supportive.
– *Ruth Devorah Zachariah, Kendell, FL, USA*

*I*n honor of the matriarch of our family, Elka Bash Bat Laike (Lillian). May she be blessed to continue to age gracefully, and may the merit of all her acts of kindness bring her health and comfort!
– *D'vira Rubin, Boca Raton, FL, USA*

*I*n memory of my mother, Devora bas Avrohom Chanina (Doris Schachne Storch) who passed away 3 Nissan, 5777.
– *Leah Gelber, Charlotte, NC, USA*

Approbations

בן ציון רבינוביץ
בלאאמו"ר זצוקללה"ה
מביאלא
עיה"ק ירושלים תובב"א

בס"ד יום ג' בשבת ז"ך תמוז תשע"ו

בין המצרים יזרח אור לישרים.

הובאו לפני גליונות מספרה של האישה החשובה מרת **הנה ברכה סיגלבאום** שתחי' על סדר פרשיות התורה, לעורר את בנות ישראל ולהתחזק בדרכי התורה והיראה, ולכל אחד יש את היכולת לחדש חידושי תורה וב"ה שזכתה לחנך ולהעמיד תלמידות רבות בדרך המסורה לנו מדור דור.

ובודאי גם בספר זה יוכלו בנות ישראל למצוא דברי חיזוק מדברי חז"ל ויביא להם תועלת מרובה וכבר אמרו חז"ל [עירובין נד.]: אמר רבי חייא בר אבא אמר רבי יוחנן: מאי דכתיב [משלי כז יח]: נוצר תאנה יאכל פריה, למה נמשלו דברי תורה כתאנה מה תאנה זו כל זמן שאדם ממשמש בה מוצא בה תאנים אף דברי תורה כל זמן שאדם הוגה בהן מוצא בהן טעם.

יעזור השי"ת שתוכלו להמשיך להפיץ תורה ולחנך התלמידות כראוי מתוך הרחבת הדעת ומנוחת הנפש וימלא השי"ת משאלות לבכם לטובה, ונזכה בקרוב לגאולה השלימה בביאת גואל צדק ולבנין ביהמ"ק בב"א.

כ"ד הכו"ח ברחשי ברכה והצלחה.

27 Tamuz, 5776

Between the days of distress light will shine for the straight,

The manuscript of *Parasha Meditations* by the important woman Chana Bracha Siegelbaum has been brought before me. According to the order of the weekly Torah portions, this book strengthens the daughters of Israel in the path of Torah and awe of Heaven. Every person has the ability to reveal Torah *chidushim* (novel insights). *Baruch Hashem* (thank G-d) that Chana Bracha merited to educate many students according to the Torah way that has been passed down from generation to generation.

Surely, also in this book, the daughters of Israel will find words of *chizuk* (inspiration) from the teachings of our Sages that will greatly benefit them.

Our Sages said, Rabbi Chiyya bar Abba in the name of Rabbi Yochanan expounded with reference to the Scriptural text: "He who guards the fig tree shall eat its fruit" (*Mishley* 27:18). Why are the words of the Torah compared to the fig tree? As with the fig tree the more one searches it the more figs one finds in it, so it is with the words of the Torah; they always yield new teachings, the more one studies them (*Iruvin* 54a).

May Hashem help you to continue to spread Torah and educate students properly through serenity and peace of mind. May Hashem fulfill all your wishes for good. May we merit the complete redemption with the coming of the Righteous Redeemer, and the building of the holy Temple, soon and in our days.

With heartfelt blessings for success,
B.S. M. Ben Tzion Rabinowitz of Biala

בס"ד

Rabbi Eliezer Raphael (Lazer) Brody
Director of Emuna Outreach

Author of *The Trail to Tranquility*, *Chassidic Pearls*, and other books

Rotem 21/9

Ashdod, Israel 77572

Email: lazerb@bezeqint.net Website: www.lazerbrody.net

18 Kislev, 5776

With Hashem's loving grace, Jewish women have been sent a wonderful gift from Above in the form of Rebbetzin Chana Bracha Siegelbaum's new book entitled *Parasha Meditations For Spiritual Renewal and Strengthening Communication with the Creator*. This amazing book is a collection of healing meditations based on the weekly Torah portion.

Rebbetzin Siegelbaum is not only a leader in Jewish education but a devout Jewish healing practitioner as well. I am happy to give my wholehearted endorsement for this wonderful new book. May Hashem bless Rebbetzin Siegelbaum with success in this project and in all her other endeavors, and may she see gratification from her loved ones and her pupils always.

In eager anticipation of the full redemption of our people in our beloved *Eretz Yisrael*,

With blessings, Lazer Brody

Parasha Meditations For Spiritual Renewal and Strengthening Communication with the Creator by Rebbetzin Chana Bracha Siegelbaum is a beautifully innovative work, soundly based upon both classical and modern authoritative teachings. *Parasha Meditations* opens the gates to the proper approach to the study of the Torah – not as a mere intellectual exercise but as a life-changing and enhancing journey, in which we engage our mind, body, soul, heart, feelings and emotions. When we approach Torah in this way, we can receive and bask in the joyous, radiant light of our Creator, in order that it may truly permeate our entire being. May the sweet waters of this wisdom spread forth to the entire world to awaken and prepare our souls for complete Redemption quickly in our days!

Rabbi Avraham Greenbaum
AZAMRA Jerusalem, Israel, www.azamra.org

Chana Bracha's *Parasha Meditations* is both a rich, scholarly text and a soothing balm for heart and soul. Each weeks' portion is thoroughly researched and brings together an array of sources and approaches from classical texts to Chassidic teachings. These insights are then blended into a remarkably healing contemplative meditation that will permeate your soul and help you apply the teachings to your daily life.

In a world where we are regrettably fed fast food 'Torah' sourced in the latest fad and dressed up in the cloak of 'truth,' hers is a refreshing, authentic - and highly actionable alternative. I thank you Chana Bracha for your teachings. They touched me deeply. And for all fellow seekers, wherever you may be along the path we collectively travel, I highly recommend *Parasha Meditations* as a companion and guide along the way.

Shimona Tzukernik, The Kabbalah Coach ®

I know Rebbetzin Chana Bracha Siegelbaum to be an outstanding educator, spiritual healer and teacher of Judaism including Jewish Meditation.

Rabbi David Aaron, Author of *The God-Powered Life and Living a Joyous Life,* Founder/Dean of ISRAELIGHT and Rosh Yeshiva at Yeshivat Orayta

Dovid HaMelech begins his book of Psalms by exploring the source of a fulfilling life. "His desire is in the Torah of Hashem and in his Torah he meditates day and night." Our sages, (*Avoda Zara* 19a), point out that when we immerse ourselves in God's Torah and absorb it – it becomes our Torah.

We don't just read or study Torah. We optimally want to soak in the Torah by meditating on its teachings. In this way, the Torah isn't relegated just to our head; it is able to penetrate our heart.

Rebbetzin Chana Bracha Siegelbaum, a leading pioneer in soulful Torah study for women, has produced a wonderful guidebook to help us bring the light of Torah into our hearts. *Parasha Meditations for Spiritual Renewal and Strengthening Communication with the Creator* illuminates the spiritual depth of the weekly Torah portion and provides guided meditations to help us integrate these teachings into our lives.

Rabbi Michael Skobac, Director of Education and Counseling @ Jews for Judaism, Canada

Acknowledgments

*T*hank you Hashem for using me to share Inner Torah
with readers from far and near.
for giving me the strength to sit down for endless hours
and letting the words appear.

Thank you for sending editors, sponsors and artists
to enhance the words with its creative look.
I'm grateful for my talented, generous, creative partners
in the third Parasha Meditation Book.

I acknowledge the Rabbis and teachers
who granted their endorsement.
Their kind, thoughtful and encouraging words
fill me with reinforcement.

Without my beloved husband, where would I be today?
His wisdom and gentle support guides me on the way.

I'm thankful for the opportunity to write
and continue to help spreading the light.

Table of Contents

Introduction

*W*hile the Book of Bereishit describes how our Patriarchs and Matriarchs endeavored to return the lost the light of Eden, and the Book of Shemot transforms this light into a holy fire; the focus in the Book of Vayikra is building proper vessels. It opens with Hashem's call to Moshe from the Tent of Meeting[1] – the perfect enclosure for Hashem's revelation. All of Moshe's prophecy in the Book of Vayikra emanated from the Tabernacle, where the sacrifices, dedicated to Hashem, channelled and rectified our will and desire. As such, the Tabernacle became the holy vessel for the love and passion between Hashem and Israel. In the absence of the Tabernacle and Temple, prayer and *halacha* (Jewish law) have become the vessels for channeling our desire for closeness with Hashem. The untimely death of Aharon's sons teaches us the importance of containing our passion for the Divine within the halachic boundary to ensure that our love doesn't turn into a "strange fire."

---

[1] *Vayikra* 1:1.

While the Exodus from Egypt is a central theme in the Book of Shemot, the Book of Vayikra builds the vessels to hold the lights of Pesach that celebrates the Exodus. It is not coincidental that we read the Book of Vayikra in the synagogue during the time-period between Pesach and Shavuot. This is the time when we count the *Omer* (referring to the daily sacrifice containing an Omer measure of barley), which enables us to build vessels for holding Hashem's light one aspect at a time.[2] As the Jewish people goes through a maturation process, this third book of the Torah emphasizes the proper balance between light and vessel through teaching how to build the Land of Israel and keeping its Torah laws. *Parasha Meditations: Vayikra* provides vessels for holding the light of each parasha point, facilitating the path toward true holiness.

---

[2] The counting of the Omer is an oral counting of each of the forty-nine days between Pesach and Shavuot. This mitzvah derives from the Torah commandment to count from the day following Pesach when the Omer of barley was offered in the Temple, until Shavuot when an offering of wheat breads was brought to the Temple in Jerusalem. Thus, counting the Omer is a spiritual preparation for receiving the Torah on Shavuot.

Introductory Blessing

I bless you to create balance in your life, and to build vessels for your own unique light.

May you tap into your personal inner spark and reveal it in your thoughts, speech and actions within the boundaries of the Torah!

May the lessons of *Parasha Meditations: Vayikra* penetrate into your mind, body and soul and help you build a life of true קְדוּשָׁה/ *kedusha* – holiness!

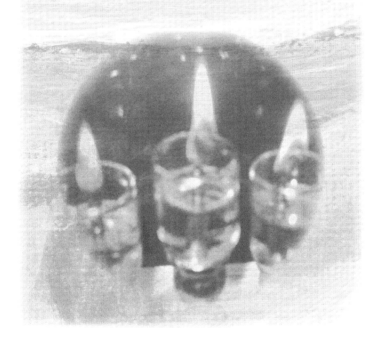

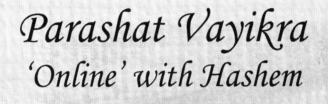

Parashat Vayikra
'Online' with Hashem

The Book of Vayikra, which means, "He called," is all about Hashem's calling to us and our calling to serve Him. Parashat Vayikra highlights proper communication with G-d. Perfecting speech corresponds essentially to refining our communication. We usually read Parashat Vayikra during the month of Nissan, which is the most opportune time to work on our speech.[3] In this week's parasha meditation, I discuss communication between parents and children as an analogy and springboard for improved communication with G-d. While we clean our cabinets for Pesach, let us work on cleaning our speech as well, so we can emerge with improved relationships in time for Pesach, which also means פֶּה-סַח/Pe-sach – 'the mouth speaks.' With Hashem's help, by the time of the Seder (ritual Pesach meal), our improved communication skills will bring us to the highest connection with G-d and our family!

Eternal Calling

This week, we begin reading the Book of Vayikra – Leviticus. Literally, the Hebrew word, וַיִּקְרָא/*Vayikra*, means, 'He called.'

וַיִּקְרָא אֶל מֹשֶׁה וַיְדַבֵּר הָשֵׁם אֵלָיו מֵאֹהֶל מוֹעֵד לֵאמֹר:
(ויקרא פרק א פסוק א)

---

[3] Rabbi Tzvi Elimelech of Dinov, *B'nei Yissaschar, Article 1, The Month of Nissan.*

22

"Hashem called Moshe, and spoke with him from the Tent of Meeting saying..." (*Vayikra* 1:1).

The last word לֵאמֹר/*l'emor* – 'saying' is extra. If Hashem spoke, obviously He would be 'saying.' Whenever the extra word 'saying' appears, it teaches us about the ongoing continuous prophecy applying to all future generations.[4] Just as Hashem called Moshe, He continuously calls us throughout the times, nurturing our ongoing relationship.

Calling – An Expression of Love

Rashi explains that a 'calling' preceded all sayings and commands. Calling with the letter א/*alef* is a message of love, an expression that the ministering angels use, as it states, "One called (קָרָא/*kara*) to the other."[5] Conversely, Hashem revealed Himself to the gentile prophets through the word וַיִּקָּר/*vayikar* – an expression of happenstance and uncleanness,[6] as it is written, "G*d happened (וַיִּקָּר/*vayikar)* upon Bilam."[7]

The Small *Alef*

The small א/*alef* at the end of the word וַיִּקְרָא/*vayikra* makes the *alef* stand out and emphasizes the difference between the word וַיִּקְרָא/*vayikra* – 'He called,' and the word וַיִּקָּר/*vayikar* – 'He happened upon.'[8] This **small** *alef* teaches us a **big** difference between the relationship of the Jewish people with Hashem, and that of the other nations of the world. The Jewish people are supposed to have an ongoing, continuous, open relationship with G*d, whereas the relationship of the gentile nations to G*d is more of an on-and-off type indicated by the word וַיִּקָּר/

---

[4] *Mechilta, Parashat Beshalach, Parasha 1.*
[5] *Yeshayahu* 6:3.
[6] The Hebrew word וַיִּקָּר/*vayikar* can mean both 'happened' and 'seminal emission.'
[7] *Bamidbar* 23:4 and 23:16.
[8] Rashi, *Vayikra* 1:1.

vayikar. The reduced *alef* also hints at Moshe's humility. He did not want to be distinguished from the nations. Therefore, Moshe was reluctant to record the word וַיִּקְרָא/ *vayikra* in the Torah, indicating Hashem's special relationship with him. An additional interpretation of the small *alef* teaches us that in spite of the greatness of Hashem's call to Moshe, it was still incomplete. Perfect 'on-line' communication can only take place when the *Shechinah* (Divine indwelling presence) dwells in its permanent home – the *Beit Hamikdash* (Temple) in Yerushalayim. It is impossible to attain the highest kind of communication with Hashem on foreign soil, outside *Eretz Yisrael* – the Holy Land, in a tent-like dwelling-place erected only temporarily for Hashem. Therefore, the small *alef* illustrates that the ultimate goal has yet to be achieved, may it be soon!

Online with Hashem
Rabbi Pinchas Winston makes the following analogy: This can be compared to using wireless internet versus an old-fashioned modem. When a person uses a modem to connect to the internet, he has to dial up the server, get into the system, and wait until all the inter-computer protocol has finished before being able to access everything from e-mail to websites. This takes time, and is not always successful. However, the beauty of wireless internet is that you are always connected. There is never a moment that we are 'off-line' from G*d. This is why halacha dictates levels of conduct and modesty even in the most private of places and moments. There is still a difference between this analogy and true relationships. Whereas keeping the lines of communication constantly open between two computers takes very little effort on our part, maintaining an ongoing, upbeat and loving relationship with another human being requires a tremendous and continuous act of will. How much more so with Hashem!

A Mother's Calling

The relationship between children and parents is a great practice for having an ongoing relationship with Hashem. A dear friend came crying to me. Her married son had called her while she was at a meeting. When she tried to return his call, no one picked up to answer. She thought that perhaps they don't hear the phone, so she continued to call again and again, frustrated that no one answered the phone. When her son finally called her back, he reproached her: "Why did you continue calling and calling? Didn't you realize when no one picked up that it wasn't a good time to call? By calling so much, you were disturbing the children from going to sleep!"

Off-line with their Mother

My friend couldn't believe her ears. "I would never do this to my own mother or mother-in-law," she told me. "First of all, I would never let them have to call again and again. And even if it wasn't a convenient time for me to talk, I would certainly pick up the phone and tell her that I would call her back as soon as I could." She explained, "This way I would save my dear mother or mother-in-law from the frustration of having to repeat calling without anyone picking up the phone. Not only did my children not pick up, they moreover had the nerve to reproach me for repeatedly calling." This mother felt hurt because her children chose to be 'off-line' from communicating with her. It is painful to reach out and not be received by another, and even rejected. I told my friend to embrace her pain and sit with it, in order to connect with the pain of the Shechinah. When our Divine Mother calls us continuously, do we pick up the receiver? Or do we let Her call and call? Hashem constantly reaches out to us, but we often chose to be 'off-line.' We can learn from this incident to be more attentive to Hashem's wake-up calls, whether through the difficulties we experience, or through becoming more aware and recognizing the Divine Supervision in our lives. Let us decide to pick up every time our Divine Mother calls!

Meditation

1. This meditation applies when we walk on the way, work in our kitchen or in the office; when we feed our children or clean our home, and prepare for Pesach etc. Whenever we are happy, and whenever we are sad, we must always remember to stay 'on-line' with Hashem. Hashem loves us and He does everything to get our attention to reestablish a connection with us. As soon as we remember, "Hashem is with me," then all is manageable, all is good. When we think about Hashem, we are actually with Him. Conversely, when we forget to think about Him, we simply disconnect from G*d.

2. Try to feel Hashem before you always. שִׁוִּיתִי הָשֵׁם לְנֶגְדִּי תָמִיד/*Shiviti Hashem l'negdi tamid* – 'I have set Hashem before me always.'[9] When you are continuously 'on-line' with Hashem you can learn to experience all the difficulties Hashem sends as a mirror for improving yourself to get even closer and strengthen your relationship

---

[9] *Tehillim* 16:8.

with Him. When facing hardships, ask yourself, "Where is the Divine spark present at this very moment? What is the message that Hashem is communicating to me right now? How can I serve G*d through this difficulty?

3. Whenever we feel challenged, we can quiet our minds, by reciting *Shiviti Hashem l'negdi tamid* in a mantra-like manner. This helps us enter into a meditative, more intuitive state, heightening our awareness of Hashem's presence. Breathe in *'Shiviti,'* breathe out 'Hashem,' inhale *'l'negdi,'* exhale *'tamid.'* Repeat this sequence four additional times as you allow yourself to enter into a very calm, centered, clear space.

4. By reciting this *pasuk* (Torah verse), we can bring ourselves into a heightened state of awareness of G*d's presence, regardless of the difficulty of the situation we are facing. The phrase, *Shiviti Hashem...* is an effective reminder that Hashem is right beside us all the time, orchestrating this whole scenario for one purpose: to get our attention, allow us to 'invite Him in' and reestablish our connection.

5. Calmly repeat this pasuk over and over again until you begin to feel even more relaxed and calm. With practice, you will feel embraced by the deep, calming sensation of Hashem's Presence surrounding you and filling you.

With every repetition of '*Shiviti*', feel your ego merging more and more with the Divine Presence. Ask Hashem in this focused state to bless you that the quality of *hishtavut hanefesh* (equilibrium), – inner calmness, and self-control – remain with you throughout your day.

6. Accustom yourself to saying, "Thank you Hashem" whenever something good happens, even something small, such as a glass bowl falling to the floor without breaking. Whenever it is hard, imagine the oneness – the small א/*alef*, from the word וַיִּקְרָא/*vayikra* always at your side, always calling you back to closeness. Eventually you will reach a place when you sincerely can thank Hashem even for the challenges and difficulties He sends your way.

7. Ask Hashem to help you transcend any challenge or difficult situation. Pray for the ability to go beyond your normal operative ego state and rise to the level of seeing Hashem in every situation. When we are 'on-line' with Hashem, there is never a moment, or an incidence, which can upset us. Staying 'on-line' with Hashem will help you learn true acceptance, because you will realize that everything is a gift, even the challenges.

8. Ask Hashem to help you anchor your newfound inner calmness and equanimity by repeating the phrase *'Shiviti Hashem l'negdi tamid.'* Whenever you need to return into this calm, centered space, repeating this Torah verse will trigger your brain to bring you back there in an instant.

Notes

We can use words spoken aloud or meditated during our morning routine as a means of re-wiring our brain. אֱמוּנָה/ *Emunah*, usually translated as 'faith,' is connected with the word לְהִתְאַמֵּן/*l'hitamen*, which means to practice. When we practice meditating on *'Shiviti...'* and speaking the words aloud, our brain will begin to associate reciting this saying with being in a calm, clear, intuitive, centered space. What is this verse teaching us that we don't already know? Any G*d fearing Jew knows and believes that Hashem is before me always. The term שְׁוִּיתִי/*shiviti* is derived from the root שׁ-ו-ה (*shin, vav, heh*) meaning equal. It denotes equanimity – הַשְׁתָּווּת/*hishtavut* – the ability to totally nullify our ego and feel exactly the same whether we are praised or insulted. Rabbi Aryeh Kaplan notes that the Divine Presence is revealed to one who has attained this level of total indifference to all outside influences.[10]

---

[10] Rabbi Aryeh Kaplan, *Inner Space*, p. 139.

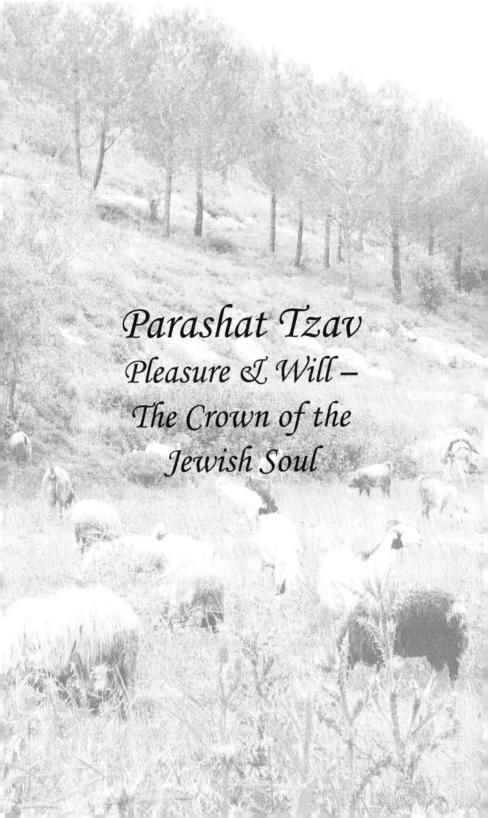

Parashat Tzav
Pleasure & Will –
The Crown of the
Jewish Soul

*I*t is difficult to relate to the Book of Vayikra, which is all about the animal sacrifices that we no longer keep. Although animal sacrifices seem very far removed from the current reality of our modern society, I found personal meaning in learning about them through Rav Yitzchak Ginsburgh's writings, which relate the sacrifices to the human psyche. Different parts of the burnt offering rectify our will and our sense of pleasure respectively. I hope this parasha meditation will be helpful to refine our will and our desire for pleasure, as part of our spiritual preparation for Pesach!

Offering the Very Best to the Creator

Learning about the sacrifices becomes more meaningful when we understand how each part of the sacrifice represents and rectifies a different part of our psyche. Of the animal sacrifice, two parts were offered exclusively to Hashem: The חֵלֶב/*chelev* – 'choice fats,' and the דָּם/*dam* – 'blood.'

חֻקַּת עוֹלָם לְדֹרֹתֵיכֶם בְּכֹל מוֹשְׁבֹתֵיכֶם כָּל חֵלֶב וְכָל דָּם לֹא תֹאכֵלוּ: (ויקרא פרק ג פסוק יז)

"It shall be a perpetual statute throughout your generations in all your dwellings, that you shall eat neither fat nor blood" (*Vayikra* 3:17).

This eternal prohibition pertains to both the person bringing the sacrifice and to the Kohen. No one may partake of either the "choice fats" or the "blood." We learn from this that the very best must always be given to our Creator.[11]

Pleasure & Will – The Crown of the Jewish Soul

The crown – כֶּתֶר/*keter* of the Jewish soul includes the super-conscious תַּעֲנוּג/*ta'anug* – 'pleasure,' and רָצוֹן/*ratzon* – 'will.'[12] Our conscious intellect and emotions are dependent on the vital energy of these two powers. Our will and sense of pleasure are represented respectively by the "blood" and the "choice fats." When a person brought a sacrifice, the blood of the slaughtered animal was first sprinkled on the altar. This culminated the first process of offering up one's will to G*d. Afterward, the Kohen would burn the choice fats on the altar. This would conclude the second process of offering up one's sense of pleasure to G*d.

Rectifying our Unconsciousness through the Sacrifices

During Temple times, when Hashem's Divine Presence was fully manifest, the Divine service would miraculously reach into our unconscious to rectify it. The process of the sacrifices thus ensured the righteousness of the Temple worshippers. Without the Temple, we cannot access the far reaches of our unconscious mind. Yet, the prohibition to eat the "blood" and "choice fats" of any kosher animal still applies today. This teaches us to continue to rectify our will and sense of pleasure to whatever extent we are able, and offer them up to Hashem. The following parasha meditation is designed to help you get in touch with your will and desire for pleasure, in order to help rectify them and give them over to Hashem.

---

[11] This section is loosely based on the teachings of Rav Ginsburgh <http://www.inner.org/parshah/leviticus/tzav/index> retrieved December 7, 2016,

[12] *Likutei Torah, Parashat Nitzavim* 49:3.

Meditation

1. Make yourself comfortable and close your eyes. Take several long, deep breaths and get in touch with how your body is seated on the chair or cushion. Feel how your breath emanates from Hashem, Who is continuously breathing through you. Visualize how your breath brings oxygen into your entire bloodstream.

2. Envision breathing through your arteries, and tune into how your conscious breathing invigorates your blood circulation.

3. Allow the happenings of your day to pass through you. Visualize all the things you have accomplished, and all those matters you didn't get to yet. Take a deep breath!

4. Get in touch with your will! What would you like to do the most if you were able? Imagine all the things you would like to do, if you only could.

5. Now, take all of these things – the manifestations of your will – and place them into an imaginary box, wrap it with beautiful wrapping paper and tie it with a ribbon. Envision placing this box in your palms facing upward, offering your will to Hashem.

6. Imagine the box disappearing from your hands, now replaced by a different gift, which you presently hold in your hand.

7. Before opening your hand, breathe deeply and get in touch with your true spiritual desires buried deep within. It could be your desire to pray, become more giving, understand truth, take on Jewish leadership, and so on. Perhaps you have been afraid to want these things, feeling ashamed or not worthy. Let any negative feelings of guilt and unworthiness evaporate away. Allow yourself to want what you truly desire deep within yourself.

8. Now, open your hand and behold Hashem's gift to you. Hashem is giving you a refined will. All the things you always wanted to want are in this present for you. Feel your appreciation of this gift G*d is giving you!

9. Now, take several relaxed breaths and allow your mind to wander to all the things you enjoy. Think about what gives you pleasure. It could be a gourmet meal, an intimate encounter with your beloved, a loving interaction with a child, or receiving a special honor or award.

10. Take those things that give you pleasure and place them in a new imaginary box. Wrap it beautifully with a nice ribbon and offer it up in your open palms to Hashem.

11. Again, your gift has been received by G*d and replaced with His personal present to you. As you unwrap your divine gift, discover the spiritual pleasures that are your true pleasures. These are the pleasures of connecting with Hashem through performing mitzvot.

12. Unwrap each pleasure one by one and allow yourself to get in touch with the warmth, love and joy that each of these spiritual pleasures gives you. Gently tap your hands and feet on the ground and table before opening your eyes to face a new, refined reality.

Notes

There are actually three points of the כֶּתֶר/*keter* – crown:

1. רָצוֹן/*ratzon* – Will
2. תַּעֲנוּג/*ta'anug* – Pleasure
3. אֱמוּנָה/*emunah* – Faithfulness

When a sheep is brought as a sacrifice, in addition to the "blood" and the "choice fats," another part is given exclusively to Hashem: "the rump," located near the tail of the sheep.[13] This third part – "the rump" – is even fattier than the "choice fats," thus it represents even more pleasure than pleasure. The Hebrew word for 'rump' – אַלְיָה/*aliyah* begins with the letter א/*alef.* The first letter of חֵלֶב/*chelev* – 'choice fats' is ח/*chet*, while the first letter of דָּם/*dam* – "blood" is ד/*dalet.* Together, these three letters spell out the Hebrew word אֶחָד/*echad* – one, representing the aspects of 'will,' 'pleasure' and 'faithfulness.' These two aspects of 'pleasure' with the aspect of 'will' form our complete oneness with Hashem. Perhaps we can say that by means of refining and offering our will and sense of pleasure, we can reach the level of emunah in the One and only G*d, to Whom all our desires and pleasures must always be directed.

---

[13] See for example *Vayikra* 7:3.

Parashat Shemini
A Vessel for the Fire of Love and Excitement

*W*e read Parashat Shemini in proximity with the holiday of Pesach, which is such a beautiful season of power and intensity. I enjoy watching how the dry tree branches awaken to bring forth new lush green leaves in just a couple of days. At this time, our love and passion become aroused together with the unfolding of nature. Therefore, on Pesach it is a custom to read Song of Songs, which describes the beauty of nature as a metaphor for the love between Hashem and His people. During the amazing period of awakening in nature, we count the Omer – a particular measure of barley. This ritual teaches us how to encase our love and desire within the proper outer measure. [14] The time period between Pesach and Shavuot is filled with the most glorious anticipation of Divine revelation. However, "the Month of Ziv – radiance,"[15] became dimmed by the mourning for the students of Rabbi Akiva who died at that time. This was because our vessels didn't quite measure up. We still lack the proper vessels to contain all of the light and love of the unfolding of spring.[16] At this time, we read about the "strange fire" that Aharon's sons, Nadav

---

[14] Barley in Hebrew is שְׂעֹרָה/*seorah* from the Hebrew root שִׁעוּר/*shiur* meaning 'measure.'

[15] The month of Iyar in which we count the Omer is called the Month of Ziv (I *Melachim* 6:1).

[16] The main work of building spiritual vessels takes place by showing proper respect, which the students of Rabbi Akiva lacked.

and Avihu, sacrificed out of love and passion. Their offering can be compared to a strong light that turns into a dangerous fire when lacking proper boundaries. I designed this parasha meditation to help contain our holy intention – 'light,' within the proper outer halachic boundary – 'vessel.'

Their Fire of Love and Excitement

וַיִּקְחוּ בְנֵי אַהֲרֹן נָדָב וַאֲבִיהוּא אִישׁ מַחְתָּתוֹ וַיִּתְּנוּ בָהֵן אֵשׁ וַיָּשִׂימוּ עָלֶיהָ קְטֹרֶת וַיַּקְרִיבוּ לִפְנֵי הָשֵׁם אֵשׁ זָרָה אֲשֶׁר לֹא צִוָּה אֹתָם: וַתֵּצֵא אֵשׁ מִלִּפְנֵי הָשֵׁם וַתֹּאכַל אוֹתָם וַיָּמֻתוּ לִפְנֵי הָשֵׁם: (ויקרא פרק י פסוק א-ב)

"Now, Aharon's sons, Nadav and Avihu, each took his fire pan, put fire in it and laid incense on it. They then offered a strange fire before Hashem, one that He did not command them. A fire came forth from before Hashem and consumed them, thus they died before Hashem" (*Vayikra* 10:1-2).

What was so terribly wrong with the act of Aharon's sons that they had to pay for it with their very lives? After all, they were holy men, and very close to Hashem.[17] They didn't have in mind to sin at all. On the contrary, when they saw the new fire descending from heaven to consume the burnt offering, they desired to add their own fire out of their excitement and love for the holy.[18] We learn this from the word וַיִּקְחוּ/ *vayikchu* – "they took," which denotes happiness.[19]

Following their Feelings without Consulting the Elders

The problem was that they did something they were not commanded to do. "They offered a strange fire before Hashem, one that He did not command them…" They took the initiative on their own to do what they thought was right, without first checking with the established

---

[17] "I will be sanctified through those who are close to me" (Ibid. 3).

[18] *Yalkut Shimoni, Vayikra*, 10, Allusion 525.

[19] Note the same word is also used to mean 'marriage,' the epitome of love and happiness.

authority – their father, Aharon and their uncle, Moshe. While some might think this is perfectly fine, G*d evidently did not approve. Inventing new ways of worship without consulting Torah authorities may be considered taking Divine service lightly.[20]

Halacha – The Vessel for Our Love

Today, in our generation of 'love' rather than 'fear,' we all too often experience the desire to act spontaneously, expressing our personal love and excitement, without first making sure that our actions are in accordance with accepted halacha. On the other hand, we mustn't become halachic robots, losing our feeling of love and excitement for the mitzvah, when discussing hairsplitting differences of, for example, exactly how many grams of matzah to eat at the Seder night within a certain time. Yet, we cannot just follow our heart by lighting the Shabbat candles, overflowing with deep intentional devotion, five minutes after sunset. While we must strive to emulate the passion of Aharon's sons, let us not forget that their lives were taken in order to teach the importance of balancing inner personal intention with correct outer action. The measurements of halacha are the vessels to contain the light of our love and excitement. Without the proper vessels, this light becomes a strange fire!

---

[20] Rabbi Moshe David Valle, top student of the Ramchal, commentary to *Vayikra* (*Avodat HaKodesh*).

Meditation

1. Sit down in a relaxed comfortable position and close your eyes. Raise your right hand in front of your face, placing your index and middle fingers on the ridge of your nose. Inhale deeply, bringing all the air into your lungs. Then, exhale completely pushing all the air out of your lungs.

2. Close your left nostril with your ring finger, and inhale slowly through your right nostril. Now, closing your right nostril with your thumb exhale through your left nostril, after removing your ring finger.

3. Breathe in slowly through your left nostril to a count of four. Then close your left nostril with your ring finger, keeping your index and middle fingers on the ridge of your nose. Hold your breath for a count of two, before opening your right nostril by removing your thumb. Now breathe out slowly to a count of eight.

4. Breathe in slowly through your right nostril to a count of four. Then close your right nostril with your thumb again. Hold your breath for a count of two. Open your left nostril by removing your ring finger, and breathe out slowly to a count of eight. Repeat this cycle (step 3 and 4) five times.

5. Put your hand down now and breathe naturally. Allow your mind to scan your consciousness for a mitzvah that you love and connect with. It could be cooking for Shabbat, visiting the sick, helping someone in need or engaging in your favorite part of a Jewish holiday service.

6. Dwell in your mind's eye on the one mitzvah you personally feel a great passion for – a mitzvah you really enjoy.

7. Now, imagine doing this mitzvah not only with your ultimate love and excitement, but also with precision and attention to detail. Note the correct timing and exact amounts, in addition to the order of the particular words you need to pronounce correctly.

8. Resolve to study up on the details of your favorite mitzvah and/or consult a rabbinic authority for fine-tuning your chosen mitzvah.

Notes

Rashi teaches us that the death of Aharon's sons took place by two threads of fire that entered into their nostrils and extracted their souls from their bodies.[21] The nostrils connect our body with our soul. Actually, soul in Hebrew – *neshamah* – shares the same root with the Hebrew word for 'breath' – *neshimah*. This is because when Hashem originally imbued the first human being with a soul, "He breathed a living soul into his nostrils."[22] By slowing our breath and breathing in a measured way, we can fine-tune our connection between body and soul – between action and intention.

---

[21] Rashi, *Vayikra* 10:5.
[22] *Bereishit* 2:7.

Parashat Tazria
Time-out for Self-Reflection and Meditation

$\mathcal{F}$ollowing the holiday of Pesach, we need to build vessels to hold the lights we received at this ultimate spiritual time. While we count the Omer, we develop our ability to hold Hashem's light, one aspect at a time, carrying it with us into our daily routine. This week of gevurah (constraint), which follows directly after the chesed (expansion) of Pesach, is especially suitable to build the necessary boundaries to hold the lights we accessed during the holiday.[23] At this time, we also move away from the expansive togetherness of the holiday to a more solitary everyday routine. Parashat Tazria teaches us about this kind of self-contained mode of reality, as we learn about the seclusion that both the birthing mother and the person afflicted with tzara'at (psoriasis) needed to undergo for their purification. Personally, at this time of the year, I work on purifying myself from all the heavy extra food I tried not to eat on Pesach. I hope you will enjoy this post-Pesach reclusive, rebalancing meditation.

---

[23] From the day following the Seder we count the *Omer*, which refers to the barley offering during Temple times. Throughout each of the seven weeks between Pesach and Shavuot, when we count the *Omer,* one of the seven emotional manifestations of Hashem is revealed. The first week during the holiday of Pesach corresponds to *chesed*, the second week *gevurah,* the third to *tiferet* etc.

Recharging Our Social Batteries

In *Parashat Tazria* we learn that a person must spend time alone in physical seclusion during specific periods of his or her life. Whenever we get out of sync, we need this aloneness in order to return physically and spiritually to a balanced state of being. This recharging of our social batteries prepares us to return to the community with joy and vitality. *Parashat Tazria* opens with eight verses describing the seclusion and purification period that women were required to go through after giving birth. Although a new mother needs support from her family and community, she also needs time alone to integrate her life-changing experience so that she may reemerge into her family and community as a new person.

The Ritual Impurity of Spiritual Disorder

The remainder of *Parashat Tazria* describes the period of isolation required of the person afflicted with *tzara'at* – a disease usually translated as leprosy, yet a more accurately translation is psoriasis.[24] This skin disease was only the outward physical symptom of a spiritual disorder or confusion. Rather than going to the doctor, people with symptoms of tzara'at had to turn to the Kohen – the spiritual healer. Only he was able to make the diagnosis of tzara'at, for which the prescribed treatment was immediate isolation.

כָּל יְמֵי אֲשֶׁר הַנֶּגַע בּוֹ יִטְמָא טָמֵא הוּא בָּדָד יֵשֵׁב מִחוּץ לַמַּחֲנֶה מוֹשָׁבוֹ : (ויקרא פרק יג פסוק מו)

"As long as the plague is in him, he shall be טָמֵא/*tamé* – ritually impure. Being impure, he shall dwell alone; his dwelling shall be outside the camp" (*Vayikra* 13:46).

---

[24] Cheyne and Black, *Encyclopedia Biblica,* Shai A, Vardy D, Zvulunov A (2002). [Psoriasis, biblical afflictions and patients' dignity] (in Hebrew). *Harefuah* 141 (5): 479–82, 496. PMID 12073533.

A Time for Silence

Today, even if we don't experience the physical symptoms of tzara'at, we certainly do not lack spiritual disorder or confusion. In our day-to-day, social-media infused lives, our continuous interaction is often on autopilot mode. We may not even be aware of our own feelings. To get back in touch with ourselves, we need to take the time to be alone with ourselves, to do the inner work that only we can do for ourselves and our souls. It may be helpful to turn to friends and family when we need support; yet, at some point, it will be time to turn inwardly for answers. When we feel confused, conflicted or in a state of imbalance, then seclusion, silence and time alone provide an essential part of self-healing.

Realigning Ourselves with Ourselves

In the Torah, those afflicted with physical tzara'at were required to be physically secluded in order to heal themselves. Today, those affected with spiritual tzara'at – confusion, worry and lack of emunah – may benefit from spiritual seclusion of meditation. Keep in mind that spiritual negativity is contagious. Whenever possible, we would do our community well by taking time out whenever we feel overwhelmed, rather than burdening them with our complaints and negative attitude.

Meditation

1. Meditation takes time. It can be hard to take this break away from all of your responsibilities. Yet, investing this time will bring more balance to your day, benefitting your interactions with others, with whom your life is intertwined.

2. Allow yourself to sit comfortably on a chair or cushion, and give yourself some moments to rebalance and realign yourself. Return your focus to your breath and see what arises. Allow your breath to raise and lower your chest rhythmically. Notice how you are feeling at this moment, paying close attention to the places within you that are experiencing discomfort.

3. Breathe into those places of pain or discomfort and notice how the tension dissolves. Imagine that your breath is like a flashlight illuminating the dark places of your soul. Allow yourself to experience this darkness, accept it and embrace it. Can you fathom what brought it about? Breathe light into any place where your spirit may feel confused and darkened. Experience how the darkness gradually flickers and turns into light.

4. Envision yourself walking alone through a dark tunnel, grabbing hold of its slippery walls and reaching the light at the end. A tall mountain meets your eye as you emerge from the tunnel. You start climbing the mountain. At first, the earth is soft and sandy, and then it turns gradually more rocky and stony. You pass rows of trees with lush, green leaves and exquisite spring flowers blooming close to the ground. Notice all their various colors and shapes.

5. Keep climbing up the mountain, while breathing rhythmically. Feel your heart beating as you continue climbing.

6. It seems as if you have reached the peak, but each time you think you have arrived at the top of the mountain, there's more distance to go. Finally, the rocky end of the trail appears. You reach the top and turn slowly to take in the entire, incredible view. Feel free to paint this picture in your mind as vividly as you would like, in all its glory.

7. You are alone – בָּדָד/*badad* and at one with G*d's creation. Being alone... being alive... feeling the greatest joys.

8. Inhale while visualizing going inwardly to the sound of בָּ/*ba*, exhale while visualizing the letters and the sound of דָד/*dad*. Repeat nine more times, and sit for a minute in silence, experiencing the Oneness of Hashem. Then walk down the mountain and return to a more refreshed and realigned you.

Notes

The Hebrew word for alone – בָּדָד/*badad*, from our Torah verse, הוּא בָּדָד יֵשֵׁב – "…He shall dwell alone…"[25] has the numerical value of ten. Ten is the number that indicates the oneness within the multiplicity. Hashem, Who is One, manifests himself through the Ten *Sefirot* (Divine emanations). Everything within our three-dimensional world includes lengths, widths and depths, each of which consisting of three dimensions as well. Length is divided into beginning, end and middle; width subdivides into right, left and middle; depth consists of inner, outer and middle. Together, the three dimensions of length, width and depth make up nine. The tenth dimension provides a space for these nine manifestations to exist.[26] Thus by sitting alone – בָּדָד/*badad*, we can experience our aloneness as part of the manifestation of Hashem's Oneness, which is expressed through the ten dimensions of בָּדָד/*badad* (according to its numerical value).

---

25 *Vayikra* 13:46.
26 Rabbi Moshe Shatz, *Ma'ayan Moshe*, p. 22.

Parashat Metzora
From Haughtiness to Humility

*P*arashat Metzora, which is often appended to Parashat Tazria, deals with the purification process of tzara'at, commonly translated as 'leprosy.' Over a century ago, Hawaiians with leprosy were exiled to a quarantined settlement in the Hawaiian island of Molika'i. The disease would at first appear as a rose-colored mark on the skin and progress into deformed limbs, weakened immune system and premature death. It was believed that leprosy was extremely contagious. Therefore, all patients were kept in strict seclusion. Even family visits took place from behind a glass wall. The patients were stigmatized as unclean and sinful beings, often ostracized by close family. Several centuries after the onset of the leprosy epidemic in Hawaii, the name of the sickness was changed to Hansen's Disease, as it was discovered that although it had similarities to the biblical 'leprosy,' it was not the same disease, and it was completely unrelated to the moral depravity that characterizes the biblical צָרַעַת/tzara'at. Although we prefer not to blame the victim, the Torah makes an exception when it comes to the disease of צָרַעַת/tzara'at. The name of the disease itself testifies that this illness stems from a serious imbalance of the soul. A person inflicted by this spiritual disease is called מְצֹרָע/metzora, which derives from the phrase מוֹצִיא רָע/motzi ra – 'emanating evil.' Although the Torah depicts this illness as a natural *consequence for someone whose entire essence had turned into emanating evil in speech and action,*[27] *there was still hope for him. Through the prescribed rectification ritual, he was able to transform into a person of the highest moral integrity.*

Arrogance – The Underlying Cause of Tzara'at

The Torah's prescription for purification from tzara'at alludes to the underlying spiritual cause of the disease:

זֹאת תִּהְיֶה תּוֹרַת הַמְּצֹרָע בְּיוֹם טָהֳרָתוֹ וְהוּבָא אֶל הַכֹּהֵן: וְיָצָא הַכֹּהֵן אֶל מִחוּץ לַמַּחֲנֶה וְרָאָה הַכֹּהֵן וְהִנֵּה נִרְפָּא נֶגַע הַצָּרַעַת מִן הַצָּרוּעַ: וְצִוָּה הַכֹּהֵן וְלָקַח לַמִּטַּהֵר שְׁתֵּי צִפֳּרִים חַיּוֹת טְהֹרוֹת וְעֵץ אֶרֶז וּשְׁנִי תוֹלַעַת וְאֵזֹב: (ויקרא פרק יד פסוק ב-ד)

"This is the ritual for the מְצֹרָע/*metzora* – the person afflicted by tzara'at, on the day of his purification; he shall be brought to the Kohen. The Kohen shall go outside of the camp, and if the Kohen sees that the afflicted has been healed from the plague of tzara'at, then the Kohen shall order two live pure birds, cedar wood, crimson (תּוֹלַעַת/*tola'at*) and hyssop to be brought for him who is to be purified" (*Vayikra* 14:2-4).

Rashi explains that the plague of tzara'at arises as a punishment for arrogance. Therefore, the rectification ritual calls for cedar wood, worm-dyed scarlet wool and hyssop, because together they allude to lowering oneself from excessive pride represented by cedar wood. Rather one must become lowly as a worm – תּוֹלַעַת/*tola'at*, and as a hyssop – a low maintenance plant that grows close to the ground.[28] The reason why arrogance brings about plagues, is that it is one of the worst character traits and it causes the Divine Presence to depart. When a person is filled with arrogance and יֵשׁוּת/*yeshut* – separate existence, he disconnects himself from Hashem, as it states: "The

---

[27] Netivot Shalom, *Parashat Metzora*, p. 70.
[28] Rashi, *Vayikra* 14:4.

arrogant and I cannot live in the same world."[29] This is because the arrogant person is so full of himself and his own existence that he doesn't leave room for G*d. Without the protective Presence of G*d, a person becomes vulnerable to plagues and illnesses. Being stuck in his own independent existence prevents him from experiencing that in truth, אֵין עוֹד מִלְבַדּוֹ/*ein od milvado* – there is nothing besides Him.[30]

Divinely Prescribed Humiliation Process

According to Rambam, "The person who is full of pride must cause himself to experience much disgrace. He must sit in the lowliest of places, dress in tattered rags which shame him until the arrogance is uprooted from his heart..."[31] The person afflicted with tzara'at, similarly, goes through a very humiliating quarantine process:

וְהַצָּרוּעַ אֲשֶׁר בּוֹ הַנֶּגַע בְּגָדָיו יִהְיוּ פְרֻמִים וְרֹאשׁוֹ יִהְיֶה פָרוּעַ וְעַל שָׂפָם יַעְטֶה וְטָמֵא טָמֵא יִקְרָא: כָּל יְמֵי אֲשֶׁר הַנֶּגַע בּוֹ יִטְמָא טָמֵא הוּא בָּדָד יֵשֵׁב מִחוּץ לַמַּחֲנֶה מוֹשָׁבוֹ:
(ויקרא פרק יג פסוק מו-מז)

"As for the person with the plague of tzara'at, his clothes shall be rent, the hair of his head shall go loose, he shall cover his upper lip, and he shall call out: 'Impure! Impure!' He shall be impure as long as the plague is on him. Being impure, he shall dwell apart; his dwelling shall be outside the camp" (*Vayikra* 13:45-46).

He doesn't only call out "Impure! Impure!" to every passerby, but even to himself when he is alone with himself. This way, he will contemplate his situation and realize that he is banished from the camp of Israel due to his arrogance that has caused the Divine Presence to depart from him.

---

[29] *Babylonian Talmud, Sota* 5a.
[30] *Devarim* 4:35.
[31] Rambam, *Hilchot Deot* 2:2.

From Haughtiness to Humility

The purification process from tzara'at teaches us that no matter how far we turn from G*d, and how much we are entrapped by the negative impulse of the other side, Hashem always gives us a chance to return to Him. The first step of the rectification is to be brought to the Kohen, for he teaches the way of humility. Since the character trait of Aharon is הוֹד/*hod* – humility, the Kohen (directly descended from Aharon) embodies humility. Therefore, he can open the heavenly gates for the afflicted to return and cleave to Hashem. The first step in the rectification process is for the מְצֹרָע/*metzora* to just be willing to come and submit himself to the Kohen. The next step is to take two pure live birds. They allude to the two different paths in the service of Hashem: first, recognition of the greatness of the Creator, which leads to humility; and second, awareness of his own lowliness, which leads to recognition of Hashem. Just as it is impossible to thoroughly recognize our own lowliness except through recognizing Hashem's greatness, so is it impossible to recognize Hashem's greatness without uttermost humility and submission. The two birds teach us that the only way to uproot arrogance completely is by serving Hashem through both of these ways together. This process is sealed with cedar wood, hyssop and worm-dyed crimson wool, which teach that if a person's heart was haughty as a cedar, he should lower himself to become like a hyssop and worm.

Meditation

1. Make yourself comfortable and relax. Become aware of how your body rests on your chair or cushion and take several deep breaths, relaxing even more.

2. Scan your day or week for episodes where you felt arrogant about a certain accomplishment, momentarily forgetting how your every achievement is in Hashem's hands alone.

3. Tune into this conceited feeling of taking excessive credit for your deeds that only alienates you from G*d and others.

4. Where does your arrogance come from? Perhaps an underlying insecurity causes your ego to hold on to greatness? Perhaps you are trying to drown out an underlying voice that cries: "I'm not good enough! I'm not good enough! I'm not good enough!" with a prideful counter-voice chirping some form of "I'm so great! I'm so great! I'm so great!"

5. Think about how wealth, beauty, health and smarts are never guaranteed for life. We exercise no control over them. At any given moment, a person may lose all of his material and spiritual attributes that makes him so proud. Hashem is in control of our lives. We didn't enter this world on our own, and we have no idea when and how we will meet our end.

6. Meditate on how every one of your good qualities and accomplishments are nothing but Hashem's special blessings for which to be grateful. Take this moment to realize how the particular achievement that made you excessively proud is a Divine blessing. Mentally thank Hashem for enabling you to reach this realization.

7. Now, tune into an episode where you felt low and unworthy. Realize how this, too, is from Hashem. Take a few deep breaths and resolve to accept Hashem's will even within your dark lowliness.

8. Imagine being a tiny drop of water in the vast ocean. Take a few breaths. Notice how you are connected to the greater whole.

9. Envision a ray of light emanating from the sun coming down to evaporate you. Imagine how you, being a tiny drop, rise up as vapor toward the sky. Visualize yourself becoming part of a cloud. Become aware of how your separate existence is melting away, allowing you to integrate into the greater whole.

10. Now, realize how your darkest moments are orchestrated from Above to eventually bring you closer to Hashem. Your talents, too, emanate from Him and are channels for His light. Thank Hashem for allowing you to become an instrument to spread His light in the world. Thank Hashem for all the great things that you do.

Notes

It is possible to serve Hashem not only when we feel enlightened but even when we are down and low, feeling spiritually impure. When we go through times of darkness and doom, when we feel far from Hashem, sunken in impurity, the main way to serve Him is through accepting Hashem's will with love. Even when we find ourselves sitting alone "outside of the camp declaring, 'Impure! Impure!'" if we accept Hashem's will at these times of darkness, this in itself is a complete rectification. In this way, we can serve Hashem through our 'lows' no less than through our 'highs.'

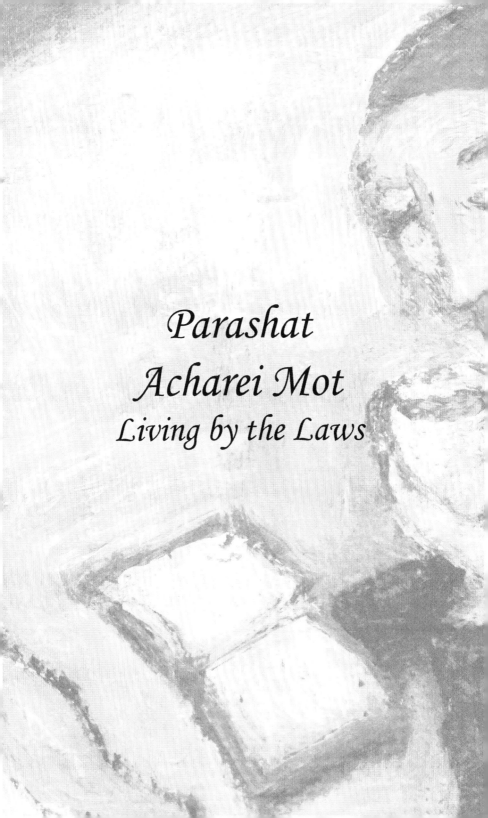

Parashat
Acharei Mot
Living by the Laws

*I*n our fast-paced society, we are often overwhelmed with so much to do that we feel we are 'running around like a chicken without a head.' At times, we add the mitzvot coming our way to the rest of our 'to-do list,' looking forward to when we can cross them off and call them 'done.' It may be a challenge to recall that Hashem granted us these mitzvot to serve as catalyzers for pulling down all the blessings and spiritual abundance that He has in store for us. Keeping this in mind helps us regard each mitzvah as a privilege rather than a chore that needs to get done. This will bring enjoyment into our mitzvah performance, which is vital for the quality of both our physical and spiritual life. In Parashat Acharei Mot, Hashem instructs us to, **"live** by the laws" and thus assures us that by keeping the Torah laws with life, vitality and love we can heal our lives.[32]

---

[32] This interpretation and the entire *Acharei Mot* section is based on *Netivot Shalom, Parashat Acharei Mot*, pp. 80-83.

Laws and Statutes as Antidotes for the Spiritual Impurity of Egypt and Canaan

The laws of forbidden relationships enumerated in *Parashat Acharei Mot* are preceded by the admonishment to refrain from the ways of both the Egyptians and the Canaanites. In the same breath, we are charged to keep both the מִשְׁפָּטִים/ *mispatim* (logical laws between people) and the חֻקִּים/ *chukim* (statutes without any known reason).

כְּמַעֲשֵׂה אֶרֶץ מִצְרַיִם אֲשֶׁר יְשַׁבְתֶּם בָּהּ לֹא תַעֲשׂוּ וּכְמַעֲשֵׂה אֶרֶץ כְּנַעַן אֲשֶׁר אֲנִי מֵבִיא אֶתְכֶם שָׁמָּה לֹא תַעֲשׂוּ וּבְחֻקֹּתֵיהֶם לֹא תֵלֵכוּ: אֶת מִשְׁפָּטַי תַּעֲשׂוּ וְאֶת חֻקֹּתַי תִּשְׁמְרוּ לָלֶכֶת בָּהֶם אֲנִי הַשֵׁם אֱלֹהֵיכֶם: וּשְׁמַרְתֶּם אֶת חֻקֹּתַי וְאֶת מִשְׁפָּטַי אֲשֶׁר יַעֲשֶׂה אֹתָם הָאָדָם וָחַי בָּהֶם אֲנִי הַשֵׁם: (ויקרא פרק יח פסוק ד-ה)

"You shall not copy the practices of the Land of Egypt where you dwelled, or of the land of Canaan to which I am taking you; nor shall you follow their rules. My laws alone you shall observe and My statutes you shall keep and walk in them; I am Hashem your G*d. You shall keep My statutes and My laws that a person shall carry out in order to live by them: I am Hashem" (*Vayikra* 18:3-5).

Why does the Torah repeat, "My laws you shall observe and My statutes you shall keep... You shall keep My statutes and My laws"? Why is the order reversed when repeated?

The Torah warns us to keep away from two negative tendencies (impure husks) – the husk of lust and the husk of idol worship, in which Egypt and Canaan were steeped respectively. The negative inclination of the Egyptians was predominantly impure lust, which induced them to idol worship as well, whereas the Canaanites' primary negative impulse was idol worship, which also brought them to lust. Through its laws and statutes, the Torah prepared a cure to prevent Israel from sinking into these two types of impurities. When preceding logical laws to statutes, the Torah aims at protecting us against the husk of Egypt, as it makes sense to abide by laws that limit lustful behavior.

Idol worship, on the other hand, is in the realm of belief without any logical reason. Correspondingly, the statutes of the Torah – which do not necessarily make sense to the human mind – are antidotes for idol worship. Therefore, the phrase that precedes the statues to the logical laws is directed against the husk of Canaan. Our Holy Torah thus teaches us that by keeping its laws and statutes meticulously, we can overcome the husks of both Egypt and Canaan – the source of all impurity and every spiritual disease.

Living by the Laws with Excitement and Vitality

Sometimes we have no energy for Torah study or prayer. It may also happen that we do not feel any enjoyment on the holy Shabbat; on the contrary, we may be counting the minutes until it is over so we can turn on our computer or smart phone. The underlying reason for losing our vitality in Torah and *tefilah* (prayer) and for disconnecting from experiencing the holiness of Shabbat is due to the influence of the two impure inclinations of lust and idol worship. Even if we don't bow down to stones and sticks, we may still run after money, medicine and doctors rather than trusting in Hashem. By keeping the Torah's statutes carefully, we eradicate any trace of idol worship and inculcate within ourselves complete trust in Hashem. Keeping the laws of the Torah, morever, helps us keep our cravings in check. This will enable us to: "Live by them [the Torah laws]" – and bring life and vitality into our Divine service. The Talmud explains, וָחַי בָּהֶם/*v'chai bahem* – "live by them" – and don't die through them. From here we learn that saving lives supersedes keeping the mitzvot.[33] Rashi, however, explains that the phrase refers to the life of the World-to-Come, for you cannot say that it means that he shall live in *this* world, since in fact everyone must die at some point.[34]

---

[33] *Babylonian Talmud, Yoma* 85b.
[34] Rashi, *Vayikra* 18:5.

"Live by them" in This World and in the World-to-Come
How can we reconcile these apparently contradictory
interpretations of, וָחַי בָּהֶם/*v'chai bahem* – "live by them"?
Keeping the laws and the statutes of the Torah will grant
us life both in this and the coming world, when we "live
by them" by bringing excitement and vitality into the way
we keep the mitzvot. We need to keep the mitzvot not only
with our full heart but also with the vigor of all the limbs
of our body, as it states, "All my bones shall say, Hashem
who is like You?"[35]

This matter is also the root and source of "live by them"
in the World-to-Come. For a Jew who observes the Torah
and the mitzvot to perfection and keeps Shabbat with all
its minutia, but doesn't feel the special עוֹנֶג/*oneg* – pleasure
of Shabbat, will also not be able to take pleasure in the next
world. Although he receives a place in the Garden of Eden
for keeping Shabbat, he will be just like a slab of wood,
without feeling the pleasure of the World-to-Come. This
is because our spiritual pleasure in the Garden of Eden,
where "the righteous sit with their crowns on their heads
and enjoy the rays of the Shechinah,"[36] derives directly
from the pleasure and vitality with which we perform the
mitzvot in this world. Conversely, the fires of *gehinom*
(hell) derive from the passion of lust for sin in this world.
Therefore, if the source of the pleasure of the World-to-
Come is the desire and excitement with which we keep the
mitzvot in this world, then "live by them" refers both to
the life of the mitzvot in this and in the coming world. By
means of keeping the mitzvot in this world with all of our
life and vitality – body and soul – we merit the pleasure to
"live by them" in the World-to-Come.

---

[35] *Tehillim* 35:10.
[36] *Babylonian Talmud, Berachot* 17a.

Keeping the Unloved Mitzvah with Our Heart and Soul
It is hard to feel excitement for the statutes, or for any
mitzvah we don't understand or connect with. Our Torah
verse charges us to keep even these tedious commandments,
solely because it is Hashem's will. Internalizing the
knowledge that we are performing the will of our Creator
gives us the ability not only to connect with even our least
preferred mitzvah, but also to perform it with utmost
pleasure and vitality. Reciting, "Blessed be You, Hashem,
King of the Universe…" can fill us with immense happiness,
as the words of our prayer testify: צָהֳלָה וְרִנָּה לְזֵכֶר מַלְכוּתוֹ/
tzahala v'rina l'zecher malchuto – "Jubilation and joy for
the mention of His Kingdom."[37] If we can be filled with
joy just through the merit mentioning, "Hashem, King of
the Universe," then imagine the infinite happiness we can
derive by performing a mitzvah with our entire heart, soul
and body, for the sake of fulfilling Hashem's will alone.

---

[37] Shabbat Morning Service, the *Nishmat* Prayer.

Meditation

1. Position yourself comfortably wherever you are sitting. Close your eyes and take a long, deep breath. Take several additional deep breaths, feeling your chest expanding on the in-breath and emptying completely on the out-breath.

2. Feel how your breath is actually Hashem's breathing through you, bestowing you with life and energy. Take a moment to sit with your breath and feel grateful for being alive right now!

3. Right now, there is nowhere to go and nothing to *do*. Right now, you are here! Allow yourself to just *be*. If your thoughts take you away to the chores that need to get done, gently bring yourself back to your breath.

4. Inhale אֲנִי/*ani* – I, exhale חַי\ה/*chai* – 'alive' – "I am alive!" Repeat four additional times.

5. Focus on one of the mitzvot that makes sense to you, one that you plan to carry out this week. It could be honoring your parents, avoiding evil speech or giving *tzedakah* (charity). Visualize yourself performing this mitzvah with all your heart and soul, and with the vigor of your entire being.

6. Place your hands on your heart and feel how it beats within you. Inhale and exhale in rhythm with your pulse. On your next exhalation, breathe warmth into your heart as you envision being engaged in one of your favorite mitzvot. You may repeat this with additional mitzvot, breathing life and vitality into each of them.

7. Now, focus on one of your less preferred mitzvot that you are called to perform this week. It could be koshering the kitchen, disciplining a child, or comforting a mourner. Visualize yourself doing one of these mitzvot with all your heart and soul, and with the vigor of your entire body, just because it is Hashem's will.

8. Recite, "צָהֲלָה וְרִנָּה לְזֵכֶר מַלְכוּתוֹ"/*tzahala v'rina l'zecher malchuto* – "Jubilation and joy for the mention of His Kingdom" and remind yourself of the importance to fulfill Hashem's decree even through these less preferred mitzvot.

9. Place your hands on your heart again and feel it beating within you. Inhale and exhale in rhythm with your pulse. On your next exhalation, breathe warmth into your heart as you envision being engaged in one of your less preferred mitzvot.

10. Envision bringing life and excitement into even this mitzvah. Recite, וָחַי בָּהֶם/*vachai bahem* – "and live by them." Inhale וָחַי/*vachai* – 'and live,' exhale בָּהֶם/*bahem* – 'through them.' I breathe life into all of the mitzvot and the mitzvot breathe life into me! Repeat four additional times.

You may repeat step 7-10 with other mitzvot, breathing life and vitality into each of them. Now, open your eyes, ready to jump into carrying out the will of your Creator with life and vitality through any mitzvah coming your way.

Notes

G*d created the world in order to bestow us with His goodness. Through sin, sadness and distress, we block Hashem's blessings from reaching our entire being. However, when we perform Hashem's will and keep the mitzvot with love and excitement, then we draw down the Divine abundance to us and facilitate the fulfillments of Hashem's will to bestow goodness to His creations. Therefore, "and live by them" is not a promise for reward in the World-to-Come, but rather a natural consequence of carrying out the mitzvot with our entire being.

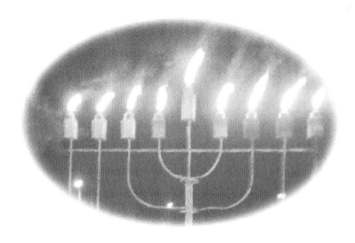

Parashat Kedoshim
Reconnecting with the
Soul of Souls

*A*t this time of the year, we celebrate Yom Ha'atzmaut *(Israel's Independence Day), which is not only a matter of national independence and security, but a spiritual milestone as well. On the fifth of Iyar, 5708 (May 14, 1948) we crossed the threshold between exile and redemption. The way is still long, but we are finally on the other side. The period of exile is behind us, and we are stepping forward on the way to redemption. We may indeed be quite far from the summit, but with the grace of G*d, the main obstacles of the last two thousand years have been removed. Now we need to infuse the physical independence of living in our Land with true love for our people. It is not by chance that the well-known mitzvah, "Love your fellow as yourself" is part of the Torah reading during the week of Israel's Independence Day. In order to establish Israel as a Jewish country that ideally reflects the Divine, we need to learn to truly love one another. The meditative practice below helps to engender and integrate love for all the people in our lives! Happy celebrations!*

Letting Go of Resentments to become Holy

In *Parashat Kedoshim* – the parasha that teaches us how to become holy – we learn about the prerequisite for holiness: "Love others as you love yourself." True holiness is not just about what we do outwardly, but it is even more about how we feel inwardly. An authentic holy person has learned to control his feelings, think only holy thoughts about others, and feel love and compassion for every creature. To be holy is to let go of all the resentments – big or small – that we may carry with us. Only then will we be able to truly love one another with a full heart as the Torah instructs us:

לֹא תִקֹּם וְלֹא תִטֹּר אֶת בְּנֵי עַמֶּךָ וְאָהַבְתָּ לְרֵעֲךָ כָּמוֹךָ אֲנִי הַשֵּׁם:
(ויקרא פרק יט פסוק יח)

"Do not take revenge, and do not bear a grudge against the children of your people. Love your fellow as yourself, I am Hashem" (*Vayikra* 19:18).

Learning to Forgive Ourselves

This Torah verse requires us to love our fellow as we love ourselves. It is impossible to fulfill this mitzvah from the Torah and free ourselves from holding on to grudges, without doing deep, inner spiritual healing work. In order to give and receive love, we need to begin by learning to love ourselves. If we don't have love for ourselves, all our relationships may suffer. Many of the women who come to me for spiritual healing have difficulty loving themselves. They may be filled with guilt and shame and have a hard time learning to forgive themselves, or they don't feel that they are good enough or worthy of receiving. I work with them to release their blocks and childhood wounds so that they learn to accept and love themselves. In order to forgive ourselves, we need to get in touch with the underlying causes of why we blame ourselves, and work on removing them. After forgiving ourselves, the next step is to work on forgiving others with all our heart, and sending them love. This, too, requires the meditative work of spiritual healing.

The Oneness of Love

The *gematria* (numerical value) of the Hebrew word אַהֲבָה /*ahava* – 'love' is thirteen. This is the same gematria as the Hebrew word אֶחָד/*echad* – 'one.' The number thirteen also alludes to the thirteen attributes of mercy.[38] Only when we become one with someone, can we really love that person. This is the essence of, "Love others as you love yourself." The greatest love is the love between a mother and her baby, since they were one while the fetus was in her womb. So how can we feel love for another who is not our child? To develop our feelings of love for a relative, neighbor, friend, or any fellow Jew we need to reveal the similarities that help us connect and unify.

Receiving Hashem's Love – the Soul of Our Soul

The body is a vessel for the soul; the soul is a vessel for the Divine. Every Jewish soul has a Divine spark of light and love emanating directly from Hashem. This is the source and power of our love – G*d's love, which is beyond our reality. Many of us cannot feel the greatness of Hashem's love until we do the deep spiritual work necessary in order to open up our heart. When we expand our ability to receive from Hashem, even in a small way, we may be pleasantly surprised at the endless love we feel.

פתחי לי פתח כחודה של מחט ואני אפתח לכם פתח שיהיו
עגלות נכנסים:

"Open up for Me an opening like the eye of a needle, and I will enlarge it for you to become an opening for wagons to enter."[39]

---

38 The Thirteen Attributes of Mercy or *Shelosh-Esreh Midot*, enumerated in the *Shemot* 34:6-7, are the attributes with which G*d governs the world.
39 *Yalkut Shimoni, Shir Hashirim*, chapter 5, Allusion 989.

Meditation

1. Sit comfortably in your chair, close your eyes and take several deep breaths. Notice anything you may be holding on to, and let go, let go... Connect with the light of Hashem, which always comes down from Above. Our body is continually filled with Hashem's light and love even when we don't see it or feel it; yet deep within, we intuitively know that we are filled with Hashem's light.

2. Imagine Hashem's light filling your head and cascading down your shoulders to the rest of your being. Envision your entire body as a lightbulb filled with light.

3. Now, allow yourself to get in touch with old feelings of guilt, resentment or other negative emotions. Did someone ever embarrass or reject you? Did you ever feel a lack of love and consideration from a family member or close friend? Did you yourself ever mistreat someone who needed you? Or do you feel guilty about something you've done? Tune into any images, words or feelings that come up for you.

4. Allow yourself to get in touch with any painful feelings that you may have repressed and swept under the rug.

5. Visualize these feelings as dark clouds within you. Can you locate these dark clouds in your body? Are there any in your head, in your throat or perhaps in your heart region?

6. Send Hashem's light and love to each of the dark clouds within you. Keep breathing into them, one by one, until you feel them evaporate or burst.

7. Think about a person that you feel badly about for whatever reason. Visualize your bad feelings/resentments/grudges as dark clouds within you, within the other person, or on an imaginary string connecting the two of you.

8. Envision Hashem's light and send it to all of these dark clouds, one by one, until each of them evaporates or bursts. You can repeat this spiritual healing exercise with as many people as you can focus on at any given time. If necessary, you can continue another time.

9. Now, send Hashem's light and love to the person toward whom you had resentment. By sending light, you can rectify your relationship with that person.

10. You may also send light to any person close to you. It could be a person that you love very much and who is in need of light and healing. See if you can feel where the person most needs this light from you, and direct your light to that place.

11. Keep sending light as long as you are able, and then ground yourself by wiggling your toes and fingers, before opening your eyes. It is wonderful to repeat this meditation daily, opening yourself to receive Hashem's light and then sending it to different people in your life.

Notes

It is important to send love to everyone, especially to a person with whom it is difficult to relate. A friend of mine once had difficulty relating to one of her neighbors. After a dispute over trivialities, she decided to work on the relationship by continually sending her neighbor love and light. One day, her neighbor sent her two *challot* for Shabbat (Shabbat bread), even though there was no special occasion. Isn't it amazing to experience the power of sending love to another person? It is so great that it can materialize into two Shabbawt challot! This powerful example proves that sending love and light can overcome tension and difficulties in our relationships – and in this case, even manifest a delightful surprise! This is what King Shlomo alludes to in his Proverbs: כַּמַּיִם הַפָּנִים לַפָּנִים כֵּן לֵב הָאָדָם לָאָדָם׃ – "As in water, face answers to face, so is the heart of person to another."[40]

---

[40] *Mishlei* 27:19.

Parashat Emor
Healing Emotions
through Speech

The entire month of Iyar is known for its healing energy, as the healing light of the sun shines brightly at this time without being overpowering. Actually, the name אִיָּר/Iyar is an acronym for אֲנִי יי רֹפְאֶךָ/Ani Hashem Rofecha – "I am Hashem your healer."[41] Moreover, the name אִיָּר/Iyar is etymologically related to the Hebrew word אוֹר/ohr – 'light.' The healing energy of the Hebrew month of Iyar is in its zenith as we approach the inner flames of Lag b'Omer that celebrate the survival of the mystical teachings in the Torah – the Kabbalah. As I write this, I'm working on channeling the special healing energy of Iyar through my spiritual healing workshops in preparation for receiving the Torah. It is amazing to experience the current overwhelming interest in Jewish energy healing. This week's parasha, אֱמֹר/Emor – 'Say' – inspired me to answer a question of one of my spiritual healing students regarding how we heal our emotions through speech.

Holiness, Life & Sanctification of Speech

This week's Torah portion is called אֱמֹר/*Emor* – 'Say.' *Parashat Emor* is juxtaposed to *Parashat Kedoshim* – 'Holiness,' through the word אֱמֹר/*emor* which infuses all of Israel with the holiness of keeping the Divine word and the

---

41 *Shemot* 15:26.

Kohanim with superior holiness because of their special holy status as servants in G*d's sanctuary.[42] In the Torah, holiness is linked with life and vitality, as opposed to death and necromancy. Whereas, *Parashat Kedoshim* concludes with the prohibition of practicing witchcraft by being a medium through the dead.[43] *Parashat Emor* opens with the prohibition for the Kohanim to become impure by having contact with the dead:

וַיֹּאמֶר הָשֵׁם אֶל מֹשֶׁה אֱמֹר אֶל הַכֹּהֲנִים בְּנֵי אַהֲרֹן וְאָמַרְתָּ אֲלֵהֶם לְנֶפֶשׁ לֹא יִטַּמָּא בְּעַמָּיו : (ויקרא פרק כא פסוק א)

"Hashem said to Moshe: Tell the Kohanim, the sons of Aharon, and say to them, none shall make himself impure for any [dead] person among his kin" (*Vayikra* 21:1).

The connection between speech and ultimate life is alluded to both at the beginning of *Parashat Emor*, which 'says' to the Kohanim to be extra careful not to become impure through contact with the dead, and at the end of *Parashat Emor*, which describes how extreme misuse of speech results in death. When the son of Shelomit bat Dibri blasphemed and cursed G*d with his speech, he was publically put to death.[44]

The Healing Power of Words

In spiritual healing, we recognize the healing power of words. In one of my online spiritual healing seminars, I taught a class on this topic and mentioned that through verbalizing emotional upheaval we may be able to heal our pains and challenges. King Solomon, the wisest of all men, taught us:

דְּאָגָה בְלֶב אִישׁ יַשְׁחֶנָּה וְדָבָר טוֹב יְשַׂמְּחֶנָּה: (משלי פרק יב פסוק כה)

"If there is worry in a person's heart, let him converse about it, and turn it into joy with a good word" (*Mishley* 12:25).

---

42 *Vayikra* 21:7.
43 *Vayikra* 20:27.
44 *Vayikra* 24:10-16.

As a therapist, I often experience that creating a space for my clients to express their distress contributes greatly to their healing process. Conversely, speaking positive words of faith and hope is another way to heal our emotions through speech. One of my students asked me to elaborate on how that works and I explained that we can recreate our reality through our speech. The power of speech was given to us as the primary way we express ourselves as human beings. At our original creation in the Garden of Eden, "G*d blew His living soul into Adam's nostrils, and he became a living spirit."[45] The *Targum* translates "living spirit" as "speaking spirit."[46] True life and vitality of the human being is expressed specifically through speech. Thus, words can create worlds as G*d Himself created the world through speech.

Healing Emotions through Speech

The choice of our words and the way we express ourselves through speech influences the quality of our life. While death is stiff and stagnant, that which is alive flows, moves and changes. Therefore, our emotions are called 'e-motions' in English, linking emotions with the motion and movement of life. The three main parts of our soul – *neshamah*, (intellectual soul), *ruach*, (emotional soul) and *nefesh* (life force soul) – correspond respectively to the three garments of our soul: thought, speech and action.[47] The *ruach* corresponds to speech, because we express our emotions through speech. We radiate life to the extent that we are able to express the emotion of love. Anger, jealousy and depression are examples of emotional blockages that block the Divine life force from manifesting within us. Through speech, we have the ability to rectify our

---

[45] *Bereishit* 2:7.
[46] Both *Targum Onkelos* and *Targum Yonatan* on *Bereishit* 2:7.
[47] See for example the Rama of Pa'no, *Article about the Soul*, part 4, chapter 4.

emotions, and thus learn to become more and more truly alive. Ramban, in his famous letter, instructs us: "Speak gently at all times."[48] This will help us overcome negative emotions such as pride and anger. When we continuously speak gently, without ever raising our voice, it becomes virtually impossible to become angry.

The Connection between Speech and Emunah

In addition to the intonation of our speech, which keeps us from becoming angry, our choices of whom to speak with and what to speak about, as well as the words we choose, also have the ability to elevate our emotions. Constantly expressing our emunah through words of praise for Hashem and appreciation for our fellows helps ingrain within us the emotion of gratitude. Gratitude engenders happiness and acceptance, which again raise our spirits, emotions and vitality. King David proclaims, "I have faith for I speak."[49] Through speaking words of emunah, we have the ability to strengthen emunah in our hearts. Nachum Ish Gam Zu of the Talmud suffered much in life; nevertheless, he would always respond to every difficulty with *gam zu letovah* – "This too is for the good."[50] By accustoming ourselves to face difficulties with words of faith and acceptance, we gradually build our emunah, happiness, and vitality.

Fire, Water and Air – The Elements of Speech

אמר/*Emor* – the name of his week's parasha – consists of the three letters: א/*alef*, מ/*mem*, and ר/*reish*. These three letters are the acronym for the three main elements: אֵשׁ/ *aish* – fire, מַיִם/*mayim* – water, and רוּחַ/*ruach* – air.[51] These

---

[48] *Igeret HaRamban*, written to his oldest son, Nachman, with the instruction to read it weekly.

[49] *Tehillim* 116:10.

[50] *Babylonian Talmud, Ta'anit* 21a.

[51] Rav Tzvi Elimelech Shapiro, *Agra d'Kala,* p. 350a and many other Kabbalistic and Chassidic writings. The element of עפר/*afar* – earth consists of a fusion of the three main elements.

elements are the expression of our emotions. Through fire, we can either express the negative emotion of anger, or elevate it into passion and excitement for the Torah and mitzvot. Through water, we can either be filled with pleasure seeking, or become calm like the soft, cool waves of a lake on a sunny day. The element of air can make us nervous, or help us rise upward in our yearning for increased spirituality and holiness in our life.

Summary of Practical Tips to Heal our Emotions through Speech
1. Overcome pride and anger by speaking gently without raising your voice.
2. Develop gratitude by expressing words of praise to Hashem and appreciation for people.
3. Whenever you face difficulties, accustom yourself to saying "*gam zu l'tova* – This too is for the good."
4. Work on making yourself happy by choosing to speak about positive, uplifting matters.

Meditation

1. Make yourself comfortable on your chair or cushion. Close your eyes and become aware of your breath, which is the expression of your *ruach* – your spirit and element of air. Place your hands on your stomach, and note how your belly rises as you inhale and empties as you exhale. Repeat this calming breath several times before moving your hands to your chest.

2. Now, get in touch with how your chest rises and falls with the rhythm of your breath, as you keep breathing softly with your hands on your chest.

3. Move your hands to your throat and feel how the air passes through, as you slowly breathe in and out.

4. Repeat the entire sequence of three breaths each of belly, chest and throat, as you imagine the Hebrew letters that spell the word רוח/*ruach* – air: ר/*reish*, ו/*vav*, ח/*chet*. Visualize the ר/*reish* as you breathe through your belly, visualize the ו/*vav* as you breathe through your heart and chest and visualize the ח/*chet* as you breathe through your throat. Feel how the entire cavity within you aspires toward spirituality and holiness as you take in Hashem's life-giving air.

5. Continue to breathe calmly as you envision yourself dipping your feet in the tranquil sea on a hot summer day. Feel how the soothing, cooling water softens your skin.

6. Allow yourself to relax and become enveloped by the calming softness of the gentle waves. You may visualize yourself deliciously floating as all worries and fears melt away. Allow the waters to penetrate any tension you may carry in your body, until each tension dissolves in the vast sea.

7. Continue imagining yourself calming down in the water, letting go of all your worries, as you visualize the Hebrew letters that spell the word מַיִם/*mayim* – water: מ/*mem*, י/*yud*, ם/*mem*.

8. Keep breathing calmly and ease yourself of any fears or tensions through the tranquil water, as you imagine the flames of the Shabbat candles. Try to visualize its blue core turning into a yellow, orange and red glow.

9. Allow the radiating flame to etch itself into your heart. Notice how it burns away any barriers surrounding your vibrant, beating heart. These barriers could include indifference, complacency or laziness. Take your time to very slowly burn away each part of the blockage, as your imaginary flame touches the circumference of your heart.

10. While you unearth and get in touch with your inner flame, visualize the Hebrew letters א/*alef* and ש/*shin* that spell the word אֵש/*aish* – 'fire.' Allow this flame to fill your entire being with bright, exhilarating, and warming light. As the flame dances within you, imagine yourself dancing with delight, while your entire being is engaged in a particular mitzvah of your choice.

11. Take several deep breaths and notice if you feel more in tune with the elements of your emotions.

ᴺotes

The root ר-מ-א *(alef, mem, reish)* appears three times in the opening verse of *Parashat Emor*: "Hashem said (וַיֹּאמֶר/ *vayomer*) to Moshe, 'Say (אֱמֹר/*emor*) to the Kohanim, the sons of Aharon, and say (וְאָמַרְתָּ/*v'amarta*) to them…'"[52] This verse is written in a different style of language than the rest of the Torah. Throughout the Torah and even in the continuation of *Parashat Emor*, the beginning of every command is written in the following style: "Hashem spoke (וַיְדַבֵּר/*vayedaber*) to Moshe saying, (לֵּאמֹר/*l'emor*), 'Speak (דַּבֵּר)/*daber* to…'"[53] Here the root ד-ב-ר *(dalet, beit, reish)* is mentioned twice while the root א-מ-ר/*amar* is mentioned only once. The triple repetition of the word אמר/*amar* in the opening verse of *Parashat Emor* may possibly allude to the three elements (fire, water, and air) that we need to elevate through sanctification of life and speech. Both life and speech characterize this week's parasha, beginning by prohibiting the Kohanim from contact with the dead, and concluding in the defilement of speech by the son of Shelomit bat Dibri. It is also interesting to note that specifically the root א-מ-ר/*amar* is used in the Ten Utterances with which Hashem created the world.[54] Originally, light and life came into being by Hashem's word אמר/*amar*. Yet, any kind of speech has power, as the magician exclaims, אַבְרָא כְּאַדְבְּרָה/ *Abra k'adabra* –"I will create as I speak!" We too, have the ability to emulate Hashem and create life with our words.

---

[52] *Vayikra* 21:1.
[53] *Vayikra* 21:17, I found this style written 41 times in the Torah.
[54] See *Bereishit:* chapter 1, where Hashem created the world in six days through His speech, described by the Hebrew root א-מ-ר.

Parashat Behar
Tuning into the
Soul of the Land

*I*t is so exciting that after having returned to the Land of Israel, we can finally keep some of the laws of the land described in Parashat Behar. Just as it is said, "More than Israel has kept Shabbat, Shabbat has kept Israel," likewise we can say, "More than the Land of Israel has kept the sabbatical year (Shemitah), the sabbatical year has kept the Land of Israel." Throughout the history of the State of Israel, we have either experienced great setbacks for our lack of keeping the laws of the land faithfully, or have been rewarded greatly for the strengthened connection with Hashem's holiness that we achieved during the Shemitah year. All the losses or victories of the State of Israel took place the year following Shemitah year. For example, the victory of the Six Day War, when we recaptured Yerushalayim and Gush Etzion, took place in the year 5727, following the Shemitah year in 5726. Keeping the laws of Shemitah makes us worthy to continue holding on to the Land of Israel. Through keeping the mitzvot of Shemitah, we strengthen our faith and trust in Hashem, while creating unity among all of the Jewish people. In this way, we become similar to the Israelites, who received the Torah at Mount Sinai in unison. It is, therefore, not by chance that we read Parashat Behar in proximity to the festival of Shavuot. I will further clarify the connection between keeping Shemitah and receiving the Torah below.

The Sabbatical Year Instills Emunah

For some people it may be difficult to relate to the concepts of the Sabbatical year mentioned in this week's Torah portion. If you live anywhere outside of the land of Israel, the only practical implication of the laws of Shemitah is to ensure that vegetables and fruits purchased from Israel have proper *kashrut* (kosher) certification. Those of us who live on the Land are fortunate enough to get a taste of the emunah that the Shemitah year instills.

An Entire Year Off from Working the Land

Historically, Israel in its essence is an agrarian society. Therefore, keeping the laws of Shemitah greatly challenged the emunah of the Israelites. While we take time off from work to celebrate Shabbat once a week, demonstrating our faith that Hashem will provide for us and sustain us, this level of trust cannot compare to the faith required by taking off an entire year from working the land.

Relinquishing Ownership to the Land

The concept of Shemitah teaches us that we never really have ownership to the land. The Land of Israel belongs essentially only to Hashem. This is why it states, "…then the land shall keep a Shabbat to Hashem."[55] We, the Jewish people, are not in the center here, but rather the land has its own will and connection to Hashem. Even if I were to weed all the thorns, work myself to a sweat turning the earth, add compost, and plant delicious grapes, as soon as the Shemitah year arrives, I am reminded how everything belongs to Hashem. "…For the land is Mine, and you are strangers and settlers with Me."[56]

---

[55] *Vayikra* 25:2.
[56] *Vayikra* 25:23.

My First Shemitah Experience

I experienced the concept of "for the land is Mine" when I looked out my window one Thursday afternoon, during my first Shemitah year on the land, and discovered – to my dismay – that my neighbor was helping himself to the most succulent grapes in my garden! I had planned to pick those grapes the next day and serve them fresh for my family and guests on Shabbat. My first instinct was to stop him, exclaiming, "What are you doing? Those are my grapes!" Then the deeper realization of Shemitah kicked in. Really, whose grapes are they truthfully? Whose land is it after all? It took some processing before I realized that all my hard work in my garden was meant not just for myself and my family but for Hashem. He gives the Land of Israel to all of the Jewish people to share and live in unison and harmony upon it, as it states: "The produce of the land during its Shabbat shall be food for all of you, for you, for your servant, for your maidservant, for your hired laborer and for the stranger that lives with you…"[57]

The Connection between Shemitah and Mount Sinai

Parashat Behar opens by mentioning that the Laws of the Land were "spoken to Moshe on Mount Sinai."[58] Rashi asks, "What is the connection between Shemitah and Mount Sinai? Behold, all the mitzvot were given at Sinai [but the Torah didn't mention Mount Sinai in connection with the other mitzvot]." The Torah does not separate between religion and the social relationships of daily living. This is why the laws of Shemitah are connected with receiving the Torah on Mount Sinai. It is explicitly through the laws of Shemitah that we implement the general principles of Torah into the details of our lives. Moreover, the laws of Shemitah engender unity among the Jewish people, which

---

[57] *Vayikra* 25:6.
[58] *Vayikra* 25:1.

is essential for becoming worthy of receiving the Torah. Thus, prior to receiving the Torah, the Jewish people encamped on the mountain in unison, "as one person with one heart."[59]

Ultimate Declaration of Faith

The Israelites expressed their ultimate declaration of faith when they readily accepted the Torah with the exclamation, "We will do and we will hear."[60] Keeping the laws of Shemitah likewise requires sublime faith, believing firmly that Hashem will take care of all our needs, even when we abstain from work in order to keep G*d's mitzvot. Through adhering to the Laws of the Land, we ingrain within our entire being that only G*d gives us the strength to accomplish anything in the world, rather than thinking that, "My power and the might of my hand has gotten me all this wealth."[61]

Freedom from Slavery

At the end of seven cycles of the seven-year Shemitah cycle, we "proclaim liberty to the land," through the same shofar that vibrated at the revelation at Sinai.[62] During this jubilee year (*Yovel*), all the slaves go free, and every person returns to his original land and family. This way, by refraining from selling the land or selling ourselves as perpetual slaves, we experience how both we and the land belong to no other than Hashem.[63] Shemitah and Yovel thus teach us to return to our essential selves and let go equally of our attachments to ownership and being enslaved by others.

---

[59] Rashi, *Shemot* 19:2, learns this from the Hebrew word וַיִּחַן/
vayachan – 'encamped,' written in singular language.
[60] *Shemot* 19:8.
[61] *Devarim* 8:17.
[62] *Vayikra* 25:9-10, compare with *Shemot* 19:19.
[63] See *Vayikra* 25:28-55.

Meditation

1. Make yourself comfortable in your space. Now, it is time to relax and allow yourself to let yourself go completely. Breathe slowly and relax even more.

2. Visualize an imaginary 'Shofar of Freedom' and prepare yourself to blow it. Inhale, and envision yourself blowing the shofar on the exhalation. The sound of this shofar will allow you to relinquish ownership to everything that is not part of your essential being. Keep blowing your imaginary 'Shofar of Freedom' several times, and let it to call you back to your essential self.

3. Crown Hashem King over your garden and home with each shofar blast. Inhale while imagining your garden if applicable. Exhale, blowing your imaginary shofar into your garden, if you have one. Now, inhale while envisioning your home, then blow your shofar into your home, relinquishing attachments to all of your possessions.

4. Repeat this sequence of breathing, blowing the shofar, and crowning Hashem over the particular possessions of your choice, as many times as you would like.

5. Now, turn your attention to your body. Blow the 'Shofar of Freedom' into your forehead, crowning Hashem there. Let the sounds of your shofar crown Hashem over your eyes, nose, ears, mouth, cheeks, and the back of your head, neck, and shoulders.

6. Make Hashem King over your arms and hands as you blow the breath of life into each of them. Crown Hashem over your lungs, heart and diaphragm, allowing the shofar to cleanse away any blockages you may be holding there.

7. Continue crowning Hashem while blowing your shofar into your small intestine, belly and colon, purifying them and making Hashem King over them. Blow the shofar into your liver, spleen and kidneys, while crowning Hashem.

8. Finally, bring the liberating sound of the shofar into your thighs, knees, calves and feet, making Hashem King over your entire being and everything you own. Keep breathing and enjoy your new freedom from attachments as you return to your essential self.

Notes

Shemitah comes to heal the land and give us a taste of the Garden of Eden, where there was no ownership or possession. Likewise, during the Sabbatical year, all the fruits of the trees become ownerless, belonging equally to all. Adam and Chava breached their idyllic relationship with the land by seizing ownership of it, instead of keeping the law of the land given by Hashem: "But of the Tree of Knowledge of good and evil you must not eat of it, for on the day that you eat thereof, you shall surely die."[64] Consequently, the land was cursed, as it states, "Cursed is the earth because of you… in the sweat of your brow you shall eat bread, until you return to the ground…[65] Thus, in order to make the land yield its produce, humanity had to give itself to hard labor. We no longer live in Paradise receiving our sustenance directly from Hashem's open hand. However, during every Shemitah year, the land gradually heals, as we learn that we are neither enslaved to working the land, nor are we its owner and master. Shemitah teaches us that we are just custodians who enjoy the privilege to dwell in Hashem's Holy Land.[66]

---

[64] *Bereishit* 2:17.
[65] *Bereishit* 3:17-18.
[66] See Avraham Arieh Trugman's beautiful article on *Parashat Behar* in his *Orchard of Delight*.

Parashat Bechukotai
Walking Upright with Hashem on the Land

*P*arashat Bechukotai is intrinsically connected with counting the Omer, which must be done in an upright position, just as the barley itself stood upright in the field. Our posture, and the way we carry ourselves in our bodies when we move through life is significant for how we look and feel. The Hebrew letter of the month of Iyar is ו/vav,[79] – a straight line which is analogous to our spine. During the month of Iyar when we count the Omer, we have a special segula (spiritual ability) to succeed in realigning our spine to become straighter rather than hunched over and bent. The more we align ourselves with the character traits that we encounter as we move through the sefirot, the more we will be able to stand erect with emunah, strongly connected to Hashem. I bless all of us to take the opportunity to work on aligning ourselves physically, emotionally and spiritually, in preparation for receiving the Torah with every fiber of our being!

The Blessings of Keeping the Entire Torah
Parashat Bechukotai opens with Hashem's redemptive blessings brought about through walking in His statutes and keeping His mitzvot:

---

[79] *Sefer Yetzira* 5:7.

אִם בְּחֻקֹּתַי תֵּלֵכוּ וְאֶת מִצְוֹתַי תִּשְׁמְרוּ וַעֲשִׂיתֶם אֹתָם:
(ויקרא פרק כו פסוק ג)

"If you walk in My statutes and keep My mitzvot, and do them" (*Vayikra* 26:3).

The first letter of the blessings in *Parashat Bechukotai* is an א/*alef* – from the word אִם/*im* – if, "If you walk in My statutes." The last letter of the blessings is a ת/*taf* – the final letter of the word קוֹמְמִיּוּת/*komemiyot* – upright,[80] which concludes all of the blessings in the parasha. Thus, the blessings begin with *alef* and conclude with *taf*. This teaches us that when all the people of Israel keep the entire Torah from *alef* to *taf* (from A-Z), the blessings of the Torah will be actualized completely.[81]

Walking Upright with Hashem in Our Land

When we reach the level of keeping the entire Torah from *alef* to *taf*, we will be worthy of Hashem's final blessing to remove all the burdens that weigh us down, which will align our posture and make us walk upright:

אֲנִי הָשֵׁם אֱלֹהֵיכֶם אֲשֶׁר הוֹצֵאתִי אֶתְכֶם מֵאֶרֶץ מִצְרַיִם מִהְיֹת לָהֶם
עֲבָדִים וָאֶשְׁבֹּר מֹטֹת עֻלְּכֶם וָאוֹלֵךְ אֶתְכֶם קוֹמְמִיּוּת:
(ויקרא פרק כו פסוק יג)

"I am Hashem your G*d who took you out of the land of Egypt from being their slaves, and I will break the bars of their yoke, and I will make you walk upright (*komemiyot*)" (*Vayikra* 26:13).

We pray for this blessing daily in our morning prayer as part of the entreaties leading up to *Shema Yisrael*, and whenever we recite Grace after Meals. At the conclusion of every meal with bread, we request: "May the Compassionate One break our yoke from our neck and lead us upright (*komemiyot*) into

---

[80] *Vayikra* 26:13.
[81] Rabbeinu Bachaya, *Vayikra* 26:13.

our land."[82] What does it mean to walk upright and why is this so important that the Torah places this blessing as the final all-inclusive blessing in the Book of Vayikra? Targum Yonatan translates the word *komemiyot* as והלכית יתכון בקומא זקופא – "I will make you walk with erect stature"[83] while Targum Onkelus translates, ודברית יתכון לחירות – "I will bring you to freedom."[84] In order to be able to walk upright with erect stature, we need to free ourselves from all fears and worries as we build our self-confidence. This blessing can only take place fully when the Jewish people live as a free people in the Land of Israel. Then, Hashem's light will shine through the Temple and melt away both our outer and inner enemies – the source of all our fears.

Walking Erect – Returning to Face Hashem

Rav Ginsburgh notices a seeming contradiction between the blessing to walk erect and the Talmudic statement that a person should not walk with erect stature:

...ואל יהלך בקומה זקופה דאמר מר המהלך בקומה זקופה אפילו ארבע אמות כאילו דוחק רגלי שכינה דכתיב מלא כל הארץ כבודו (תלמוד בבלי מסכת ברכות דף מג/ב)

"...One should not walk with erect stature, since Mar said: If one walks with erect stature even for four cubits, it is as if he pushed against the heels of the Divine Presence, since it is written, 'The whole earth is filled with His glory.'"[85]

According to the Talmud, walking with erect stature is a sign of arrogance, pushing ourselves forward, as if our head pushes away Hashem's feet from above us. Rav Ginsburgh solves this contradiction by explaining that there are two different kinds of relationships with Hashem. The Babylonian Talmud depicts the relationship during exile,

---

[82] ברכת המזון – Grace After Meals.
[83] Targum Yonatan ben Uziel, Ibid.
[84] Targum Onkelos, Ibid.
[85] *Yesha'yahu* 6:3; *Babylonian Talmud, Berachot* 43b.

when we experience G*d's Presence primarily above our head. However, during the Messianic era, we will once again experience Hashem's Presence face-to-face – in front of us, as King David described, "I have set Hashem before me always."[86] We will then return to the relationship with Hashem that the first man and woman experienced in the Garden of Eden.[87]

The Spiritual Height of the First Human Beings

A different Talmudic interpretation of the word קוֹמְמִיּוּת/ *komemiyot* coincides with this concept. "Rabbi Meir says: '*Komemiyot* refers to the two *komot* (statures) of the first human being.'"[88] Adam and Eve were originally created much 'taller' than people are today. Their spiritual height enabled them to be, so to speak, 'eye to eye' with Hashem. Our relationship with G*d is evolving toward this level of spiritual height, where Hashem's Presence is *before* us rather than *above* us. Therefore, the blessing that G*d will lead us upright refers to the Messianic era, when walking upright no longer will be "pushing against the heels of the Divine Presence," since we will experience Hashem's Presence primarily before us at eye level, rather than above our head.

Hashem Walking Among Us as in the Garden of Eden

In this week's parasha, prior to the blessing that G*d will lead us upright, He promised us that He would walk among us:

וְהִתְהַלַּכְתִּי בְּתוֹכְכֶם וְהָיִיתִי לָכֶם לֵאלֹהִים וְאַתֶּם תִּהְיוּ לִי לְעָם:
(ויקרא פרק כו פסוק יב)

"I will walk among you and will be your G*d and you shall be my people" (*Vayikra* 26:12).

---

[86] *Tehillim* 16:8.
[87] Rav Yitzchak Ginsburgh, Video class, "Seeing Eye to Eye with God" <http://www.inner.org/parshah/leviticus/bechukotai/seeing-eye-eye-god.php> retrieved December 30, 2016.
[88] *Babylonian Talmud, Sanhedrin* 100b and *Baba Batra* 75a.

Rashi depicts the idyllic scene of the renewed relationship with G*d that this blessing implies: I WILL WALK AMONG YOU – "I will, as it were, walk with you in the Garden of Eden, as though I were one of yourselves and you will not be frightened of Me..."[89] In order to truly walk upright without fear, we need to return to our original relationship with Hashem in the Garden of Eden. While we anticipate Hashem's Presence to finally return and reside in the Temple, we can empower ourselves to rehearse Hashem's promise "to make us walk upright" by meditating ourselves into a redemptive 'eye-to-eye' relationship with Him.

---

[89] Rashi, Ibid.

Meditation

1. This meditation is a walking meditation that can be practiced at any time, whether outdoors or even inside your home while moving from one room to the other. Start by standing upright and become aware of your posture. What is the shape of your spine? How does it feel? Is it easy or challenging to hold yourself upright? Are your shoulders slouching, or is your neck sloping forward?

2. Stand against a wall and allow the back of your head, shoulders, elbows and the back of your heels to touch the wall. Rock your tailbone down and tilt your pelvis slightly upward, feeling your belly drawing inward. Feel the four corners of each foot firmly pressing against the floor.

3. Take slow deep breaths. Feel your lungs expanding and your chest rising.

4. Focus on the parts of your body that feel misaligned. Which emotions are you holding onto in these body parts that manifest as resistance to your standing upright? Is it a lack of self-confidence that makes your shoulders slouch? Perhaps there are fears preventing you from standing erect?

5. Close your eyes and envision Divine light in front of you. Take a few breaths.

6. Open your eyes and imagine Hashem's Presence before you. Mentally send Hashem's light into the parts of you that resist standing upright. As you inhale, feel your spine lengthening, as if a string from above were pulling you upward to an erect posture.

7. Now, begin to walk slowly as upright as you can, while still feeling flexible and free. As you walk, keep imagining an invisible string pulling you upward, seeing Hashem's perpetual Presence before you.

8. Open your mouth and speak to Hashem as a person speaks to his friend. Tell Him about your challenges in aligning yourself and standing completely upright.

9. Ask Hashem to remove all fears and anything else that is weighing you down.

10. When you have completed your walk, notice how you have come one step closer to experiencing: "I will break the bars of their yoke, and I will make you walk upright."[90]

---

[90] *Vayikra* 26:13.

Notes

Walking upright with Hashem can be manifested in the physical, spiritual and emotional realms. As we have recently entered the redemption process, we have begun to align ourselves in all of these realms. The Alexander Technique, which teaches ease of movement through lengthening the spine and becoming upright, was developed in our time.[79] Moreover, many individuals in our generation are working hard to align themselves emotionally through various kinds of therapy and spiritual healing, and through the worldwide *Ahavas Yisroel* Project.[80] In the spiritual realm, there is a shift from relating to Hashem as a punishing G*d above one's head, toward relating to Hashem more like a 'friend' as we become more connected with *Ahavat Hashem* – (love of G*d). This is why Rabbi Nachman's teaching about "talking to Hashem like you'd talk to your best friend" has gained such popularity in recent times. The empowering blessings in our Torah portion are on the verge of being fulfilled as we approach the zenith of redemption when G*d will tell us: "…call me *Ishi* (my husband), and do no longer call me *Ba'ali* (my master)!"[81]

---

[79] The Alexander technique was invented by F.M Alexander, Australia, 1869-1955.
[80] For more info about the Women's *Ahavas Yisroel* Project see <http://www.ayproject.com/>.
[81] *Hoshea* 2:18.

Epilogue

$\mathcal{T}$he Book of Vayikra is about establishing true relationships both with other people and with G*d, following the example of Moshe, our teacher, who reached the ultimate relationship with Hashem. The foundation of a good relationship is good communication. Thus, the Book of Vayikra opens with Hashem's calling to Moshe from the Tent of Meeting, expressing His love and desire for an ongoing, continuous, open relationship with Moshe and the Jewish people. This relationship can only be consummated in the Holy Land, when our glorious Temple in Jerusalem will provide a permanent abode for Hashem's presence on earth. A sacrifice in Hebrew – קָרְבָּן/*korban* means 'to bring close.' It is therefore not coincidental that the sacrifices occupies a central place the Book of Vayikra, which is about rectified relationships. In *Parashat Shemini*, the sons of Aharon overstepped their boundaries in their desire for closeness with Hashem, teaching us an eternal lesson of balancing inner personal intention with correct outer action. Moreover, they lacked the interpersonal skills needed to get married[82] and to respect their elders.[83] Arrogance alienates us both from Hashem and from

---

[82] *Yalkut Shimoni Vayikra* 10:524.
[83] *Midrash Tanchuma Acharei Mot,* chapter 6.

other people.[84] It causes us to destroy our relationships by evil speech, which in Biblical times, led to the illness of tzara'at as expounded in the Torah portions of *Tazria* and *Metzora*. The rectification for this spiritual disease is for the afflicted to go into temporary seclusion in order to reflect in solitude and relearn how to relate properly to others. The purification process from tzara'at inculcates humility. If a person's heart was haughty as a cedar, he should lower himself like a hyssop and worm. Yet, no matter how far he may have strayed, Hashem always gives a chance to repent. Whereas *Parashat Acharei Mot* focuses on the forbidden relationships from which we must refrain, *Parashat Kedoshim* highlights perfecting our interpersonal relationships, the prerequisite for our relationship with G*d. Our speech – the central theme of *Parashat Emor* is our main vehicle of communication through which we rectify every relationship. Perfected relationships includes sharing our possessions and the fruits of our land as the laws of Shemitah instruct us in *Parashat Behar*. Furthermore, in order to facilitate a true personal relationship, no Jew may remain a permanent slave, thus we must set every Jewish slave free at the Yovel year. Finally, when we have gained complete freedom from both our external and internal enemies, then we are ready to form the highest and deepest relationship with Hashem and walk upright eye-to-eye with G*d in our Holy Land, as expounded on in the final parasha of the Book of Vayikra. I have faith that this third book of *Parasha Meditations* will help bring us closer to consummate such relationship.

---

[84] *Babylonian Talmud, Sota* 5a.

Parasha Meditations: For Spiritual Renewal and Strengthening Communication with the Creator includes:

BOOK ONE:
BEREISHIT *Stepping Inward Toward the Hidden Light*

BOOK TWO:
SHEMOT *Internalizing Healing Transformation*

BOOK THREE:
VAYIKRA *Online with Hashem*

BOOK FOUR:
BAMIDBAR *Visualizing our Lives' Journeys*

BOOK FIVE:
DEVARIM *Integrating Torah from Top to Toe*

For further information and recordings, please contact info@berotbatayin.org

About the Author

Rebbetzin Chana Bracha Siegelbaum, a native of Denmark, is Founder and Director of *Midreshet B'erot Bat Ayin: Holistic Torah for Women on the Land,* emphasizing women's spiritual empowerment through traditional Torah values. She is the author of *Women at the Crossroads: A Woman's Perspective on the Weekly Torah Portion, Ruth: Gleaning the Fallen Sparks, The Seven Fruits of the Land of Israel with their Mystical & Medicinal Properties,* which won three awards, and a children's book, *The Nameless Chicken from Judea.* Her latest book series, *Parasha Meditations For Spiritual Renewal and Strengthening Communication with the Creator: Bereishit* and *Shemot,* was released in 2016. Chana Bracha has a married son and several granddaughters, and lives with her husband and younger son on the land of the Judean Hills, Israel.

Rebbetzin Chana Bracha Siegelbaum serves as a powerful role model for women of all ages from the four corners of the world, including girls who grew up in observant Jewish homes, those in the process of returning to Torah, and women converting to Judaism. Through the Rebbetzin's unique Torah from a woman's perspective, together with her wisdom and spiritual insight, she helps ignite the spark in the neshamah of each woman who seeks her guidance. Rebbetzin Chana Bracha practices EmunaHealing as a highly impactful way to fulfill the Torah commandment to "Love your fellow as yourself..." A gifted teacher and devout Jewish healing practitioner, Rebbetzin Chana Bracha imparts blessing and light to women who turn to her for Torah learning, spiritual growth and healing.

About the Artist

Yenta Leah Guzzi started painting professionally when she returned to Torah and realized that anyone who doesn't believe in Hashem should just try painting an apple! She currently teaches art classes and is exhibiting her art in the greater Jerusalem area. Yenta Leah is deeply inspired by the amazing beauty of the spiritual landscapes in Israel. She lives in Bat Ayin and is grateful to be included in this most inspiring book.

Her paintings are exhibited at http://yentaleah.gallery.

About Midreshet B'erot Bat Ayin

Midreshet B'erot Bat Ayin: Holistic Torah for Women on the Land, envisaged in 1996 by Rebbetzin Siegelbaum, is situated in the heart of the Judean Hills in Israel. Here, women of all backgrounds and ages receive nourishment for mind, body & soul by integrating textual Torah study – Bible, Jewish Law, Prayer, Jewish Mysticism and Chassidism with cultivation of the Land of Israel, creative spiritual expression and healthy living. For more information and to apply: www.berotbatayin.org, info@berotbatayin.org.

For more information about *Midreshet B'erot Bat Ayin: Holistic Torah for Women on the Land*, additional publications by Rebbetzin Chana Bracha, and dedication opportunities, please contact us at info@berotbatayin.org

About EmunaHealing

If you enjoyed *Parasha Meditations*, you may be interested in taking EmunaHealing courses and experiencing private EmunaHealing sessions with Rebbetzin Chana Bracha Siegelbaum. EmunaHealing is a Torah-based system of spiritual healing that teaches us to unblock negative energy and access Hashem's healing light within. By going through the deep EmunaHealing process, every precious neshamah can truly connect with Hashem's light. EmunaHealing facilitates spiritual renewal, strengthening our connection with the Creator by removing the exterior layers (*klipot*) that block Hashem's life-giving energy from flowing freely within our entire being – our organs, emotions and psyche. EmunaHealing teaches us to let go and allow Hashem to run our lives, while consciously choosing life, light and closeness to Him. In this way, we can finally connect with and reveal our true Divine inner light.

EmunaHealing – Jewish Spiritual Healing from the Torah aims to remove any negative energy from blocking our energy fields or auras, and infuse Divine light into the body, mind and soul of every woman we treat. During each EmunaHealing session, Hashem guides us to understand the root of the problems and ailments. Then, with focused prayer (tefilah) and energy work, we remove spiritual and emotional blockages that stand in the way of healing. Strengthened by guided imagery and insightful counseling, each woman is further empowered to overcome her fears and insecurities in order to incorporate healthy changes into her daily routine.

For more information, to register for a course or to book a session, www.berotbatayin.org/emunahealing/ or email: emunahealing@berotbatayin.org

Glossary

Aliyat neshamah: Spiritual elevation for the soul – acts of benevolence done on behalf of someone who passed away in order to elevate the soul of the departed in the World-to-Come.

Aharon: Aaron the Kohen

Beit Hamikdash: The glorious Temple in Jerusalem

Bereishit: Genesis; literally, 'in the beginning.' The Book of Bereishit is the first book of the Torah.

Bubby: Yiddish for grandmother

Challot: Shabbat bread

Chassidic: Pertaining to Chassidism, a branch of Judaism founded by Rabbi Yisrael Ba'al Shem Tov, emphasizing spirituality through deep connection and popularization of the inner dimensions of the Torah. The word Chassid/ic is related to the Hebrew word for loving-kindness and piety.

Chesed: Loving-kindness; fourth of the Ten Sefirot

Emunah: Faith; an innate conviction and perception of eternal truth

Eretz Yisrael: The Land of Israel

Gematria: Numerical value

Gevurah: Power, restraint; fifth of the Ten Sefirot

Halacha: Jewish Law

Hashem: G*d; literally, 'The Name'

Hod: Glory, humility, sincerity and acknowledgement; eighth of the Ten Sefirot

Iyar: Hebrew month corresponding to April/May.

Keter: Crown; first of the Ten Sefirot

Klipah/Klipot: Shell/s; in Kabbalah – spiritual shell/s that hide/s G*d's light

Kohen/Kohanim: Priest/s; literally from the word 'to serve'

Lag b'Omer: Literally, the thirty-third day of the Omer sacrifice of barley which takes place between Pesach and Shavuot. Lag b'Omer commemorates an interruption or end of the plague that killed twenty two thousand students of Rabbi Akiva.

Midrash: Homiletic interpretation of the Torah, from the root 'to seek out' or to investigate the deeper meaning between the lines.

Mikdash: Sanctuary, holy place

Mitzvah/Mitzvot: Divine commandment/s

Moshe: Moses

Nefesh: Lowest part of the soul (animal soul); connected with the body

Neshamah: Divine (intellectual soul); literally, 'breath of life'

Nissan: Hebrew month corresponding to March/April.

Parasha/t: Torah portion; one of the fifty-five weekly Torah sections read annually in the synagogue, through rotation of a weekly parasha.

Pasuk: Torah verse

Pesach: Passover

Ruach: Spirit (emotional soul)

Seder: Literally, 'order,' a ceremonial meal including recital of the Haggadah, (the story of the Exodus from Egypt), and eating symbolic foods. Keeping the Pesach Seder is a halachic requirement. The Sephardic tradition includes a Rosh Hashana and Tu b'Shevat Seder.

Sefirah/Sefirot: Divine emanations or manifestations within creation. The sefirot serve as an interface between G*d's infinite light and the physical reality we experience. They are G*d's imprint in the world – His attributes for us to emulate in order to reflect being created in His image.

Shavuot: Pentecost, celebrating the giving of the Torah on Mount Sinai

Shechinah: Divine Feminine Indwelling Presence

Shema Yisrael: (Sometimes shortened to simply *Shema*), the first two words of שְׁמַע יִשְׂרָאֵל הָשֵׁם אֱלֹהֵינוּ הָשֵׁם אֶחָד /*Shema Yisrael Hashem Elokeinu Hashem Echad* – "Hear, O Israel: Hashem is our G*d, Hashem is one" (*Devarim* 6:4). This Torah verse serves as one of the most important morning and evening prayers that encapsulates the monotheistic essence of Judaism.

Shemitah: The Sabbatical year for the land

Shemot: Exodus; literally, 'names,' The Book of Shemot is the second book of the Torah.

Shofar: Ram's horn

Talmud: The authoritative body of Jewish law and narrative comprising the Mishnah and the Gemarah c. 500 CE; a commentary on the Mishnah; literally, 'instruction.'

Tefilah: Prayer

Tehillim: Psalms

Tiferet: Harmony, beauty, compassion; sixth of the Ten Sefirot

Torah: Refers to the Five Books of Moses, but extended to include the entire body of Jewish teaching; literally, 'teaching.'

Tzara'at: A spiritual disease usually translated as leprosy, yet is more accurately translated as psoriasis.

Tzedakah: charity

Yovel: The Jubilee year, the fiftieth year after seven shemitah cycles

Zeideh: Yiddish for grandfather

Made in the USA
Middletown, DE
16 February 2023

25003348R00077